Art Clay
Silver & Gold

18 Unique Jewelry Pieces

to Make in a Day

Jackie Truty

Published by

To place an order or obtain a free catalog, please call 800-258-0929.

Library of Congress Catalog Number 2003114193
ISBN 0-87349-557-8

Edited by Christine Townsend

Designed by Jon Stein

Dedication

To my incredible husband, Tom,

who after 25 years still

hasn't learned to say no.

Acknowledgments

This book, the first in a long line, I hope, has been a long time coming. It was only possible with the help of the many Art Clay Instructors whose contributions grace these pages. It is their generosity and hard work that have given this book its unique and appealing designs. I thank Patricia, Judi, Maria, Debbie, Johnna, Leighton, Arlene, Julie, and Jane from the bottom of my heart.

I also want to thank Seigo Mukoyama, CEO, partner and friend, for his faith, sacrifice and patience. He has adapted to Chicago's un-Tokyo-like weather (and winter) with stoic perseverance and often disbelief. I have come to appreciate his honesty, humor, and calmness as welcome ingredients in an otherwise stress-filled mix, and I look forward to the level of success that Art Clay World, USA will achieve because of his dedication and commitment.

Lastly, I would like to thank Aida Chemical Industries, LTD., and Aida-san in particular, for its (and his) support and confidence in Art Clay World, USA. Of course the inspiration has been, and will continue to be, Art Clay Silver itself, and we have our own high level of confidence in its bright (pun very much intended) and shiny future.

Contents

Introduction

In the beginning, there was Aida Chemical Industries, a family-run business in Tokyo, Japan. Since 1963, Aida had been in the successful business of recycling precious metals: silver, from exposed photography, medical and veterinary film; gold, from electronics and post-mortem dental work. There certainly was enough film to recycle—rooms of it, warehouses of it—all being reclaimed, emulsified, and reformed into new, pure silver ingot.

In 1991, Aida Chemical Industries applied for a development patent. Soon after, Art Clay™ was born. Between 1991 and 1994 the various types of clay, materials, and specialty tools were developed. A specific Division of Aida Chemical Industries—DAC—was established in 1994, specifically for the Art Clay business. DAC is an acronym for D (dream and development), A (aggressiveness and ambition) and C (creativity and [ecologically] clean).

Art Clay was introduced to the United States in 1997 through Paragon Industries and Swest Corporation. In 2000, Aida Chemical Industries decided to open its own offices, Art Clay USA, Inc., in Torrance, California. Then, in November 2001, despite increasing sales and a widening customer base, downturns in the Japanese economy forced Aida Chemical Industries to consider closing its offices in the United States. After careful consideration, Art Clay USA, Inc. became Art Clay World, USA, and moved its offices, inventory, and operations to the Chicago area under new management.

Old, exposed film ready for emulsification.

There have been many changes since then—new growth, expansion, and innovation. However, Aida Chemical Industries' and DAC's creative philosophy remains unchanged. According to Art Clay's Mission Statement, "The philosophy behind Art Clay World encompasses four purposes—creativity, freedom, equality, and peace of spirit …

"The 'joy of creativity' using Art Clay Silver is reflected in its many forms from jewelry, accessories, and art objects. Art Clay World acknowledges and respects the creativity of both instructors and users, and actively promotes their freedom of expression. Activities of all members are welcome and accepted equally. We use the purity of our silver to symbolize the purity of the creative spirit among members and users and to promote our motto: harmony, cooperation, and peace."

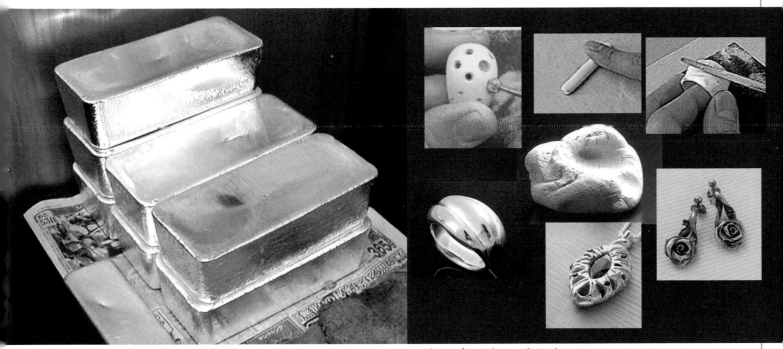

Pure silver ingot from recycled film.

One lump of Art Clay—unlimited variety.

While this philosophy may seem "hokey" to some, especially in the West, it is important to remember that in Japan, it is taken very seriously: "In adapting the original Japanese curriculum for the North American market, we felt it essential that we keep the spirit and intent of the program. The timeline could be compressed, projects adapted, and tools substituted, but we knew that the importance of good technique and the focus on perfecting those techniques through education could not be de-emphasized. We felt that the creativity of our customers, students, and instructors could best be served by providing them with thorough, concise education. Once the individual techniques of working with Art Clay were learned and mastered, students then would be free to focus on their creative spirit."

Art Clay Silver isn't like any other medium. It has similarities to ceramics, polymer clay, and traditional metalworking, but is different enough to cause confusion and frustration in the most experienced artists unfamiliar with its unique characteristics. It is 99.9 percent pure silver in 1-to 20 micron-sized particles, mixed with a non-toxic cellulose-based organic binder and water. Though it looks and works much like other clays, it is air-sensitive and must be kept moist in order to shape it. While wet, Art Clay can be stamped, rolled, used with texture plates and molds, and sculpted. Once completely dry, Art Clay's versatility and easy workability really shine. While in the greenware state (akin to unfired ceramic greenware), Art Clay can be filed, engraved, drilled, and sanded to the desired detail—and all the residue is recyclable. You can add additional clay at any time before *and* after firing. But the most amazing aspect of using Art Clay is evident after firing. You can polish Art Clay to a brilliant, mirror finish in just minutes, using such traditional polishing methods as sandpaper, a polishing wheel, or mini-power tools. In fact, fired Art Clay Silver has the strength of 18k gold.

This book serves both the newcomer and the experienced metal clay artist. It offers essential, basic information about Art Clay Silver and Gold products, materials, and tools, along with projects at the beginning and advanced levels. It is also about what makes Art Clay Silver and Gold different, easy, and fun to use. And it is about thinking "outside the box," freeing your imagination, and providing the techniques and tools to allow your creative spirit free reign. We invite you to join us in celebrating this new and exciting medium. Enjoy!

Chapter One

The Basics...
How Many Ways Can You Say Clay?

In its clay state, Art Clay is sensitive enough to retain fingerprints.

Art Clay comes in many consistencies and several special forms. Each has its own use, and all but one are aqueous (water-soluble) solutions consisting of micron-sized particles of silver, a cellulose-based organic binder, and water.

- After firing, **all** Art Clay Silver types are reduced to 99.9 percent fine silver, and can be stamped (hallmarked) as such by the artist.
- Art Clay Silver Clay Types can be rolled, pressed into moulds, textured with stamps and plates, and sculpted.
- Except for Art Clay Silver 650, all shrink 9 percent to 10 percent when fired.
- The maximum firing temperature of the Regular and Slow Dry Types clay, syringes, and paste is 1600°F for 10 minutes, or 1472°F for 30 minutes.
- Pure silver wire can be fired with any of the Art Clay Silver types, and sterling can be used with ACS 650 Low Fire.
- Certain gemstones with a Mohs* hardness of 7.5 or higher can be fired in place with Art Clay Silver Standard and Slow Dry. These include ruby, sapphire, spinel, cubic zirconium, and some heat-diffusion topaz. Add chrome diopside, moonstone, all garnets, and obsidian when using 650 Low Fire clay.

Art Clay Regular

Art Clay Regular has a consistency that most resembles polymer clay, or piecrust dough. It comes in 10gm, 20gm, 50gm, and 100gm packages. There is an inner plastic package and an outer package. The shelf life of the clay type is five years, unopened.

Clay Type—same packaging, different weight.

Once opened, the clay type is susceptible to the air and must be kept moist in order to retain is pliability and workability. The time the clay takes before it begins to dry depends on the ambient climate. In humid environments such as Florida, very little additional moisture may be needed. However, in arid climates such as Nevada and parts of Utah, humidifiers, or similar steps may be necessary in order to keep the clay workable. Here are some suggestions:

- As soon as the inner package is opened, put the clay between two moistened paper towels. Return all clay to this spot when not in use. Keep the towels moist at all times.
- Put all unused clay in re-sealable plastic bags.
- Use a "claykeeper" or similar jar that contains a moistened sponge. This will provide the humidity without creating a slimy mess!
- Keep a fine spray bottle handy and "mist" the clay between uses.
- Have a nearby personal humidifier constantly adding moisture to your work area.

In any event, you'll want to keep a small paintbrush and a container of water handy at all times to dampen any areas of your clay surface that show unwanted cracking.

Art Clay Paste Type

This type comes in a screw top jar in 10gm, 20gm, and 50gm quantities. The only difference between Paste Type and Clay Type is the amount of water in the mixture. Paste type comes in the consistency of yogurt and most people dilute it further to the consistency of thick cream. It's used in several ways:

Boxes are color-coded for easy identification.

- As a glue to join two pieces of dry or wet clay together. This is a vital function, since a very solid bond is necessary for a permanent joint after firing.
- As a gap filler for cracks and pits that appear in dried pieces.
- To attach fine silver findings, such as bailbacks or brooch tabs to dried or wet clay pieces. During firing, the normal shrinkage of the clay permanently bonds the findings to the Art Clay Silver piece. This eliminates the need to solder or glue findings after firing.
- When applied in separate layers onto organic forms such as leaves, pods, dried flowers, etc, the Paste Type creates a perfect impression of that form. During firing, the organic material burns away, leaving the original impression in the silver which can then be polished to the desired finish.

(A) = Syringe type A < with 1 tip>

(B) = Syringe type B < with 3 tips>

No sticker = Syringe type <without tip>

Syringe Type

Syringe Type is 10gm of Art Clay Silver in a pre-filled syringe. Syringe Type comes packaged three ways: with color-coded tips, each an increasingly larger diameter; a one-tip (green) nozzle; and without any tips at all, purely a refilled syringe. Each of the tips is reusable and only need be purchased once. The consistency of Syringe Type is totally different from that of Paste Type, i.e., it's not paste in a syringe. Syringe Type is thicker, more controllable. It can be used in a variety of ways:

• As a repair glue, like spackle, to fill cracks and gaps.
• To attach findings to wet or dry clay pieces.
• To decorate pieces, much like using cake decorating tips. Lines, filigree, faux cloisonné borders, and even balls can be created with Syringe Type. Most people can master the use of the syringe with just a few tries. Others need longer to learn the hand/eye control necessary to produce perfect beads of clay.

In addition to these three basic consistencies, Art Clay Silver comes in several unique varieties. Each has a special use and purpose.

Art Clay Slow Dry

As its name suggests, this clay type was formulated to remain pliable for up to five times longer than the regular clay. It is packaged in the same sizes as Standard Type. When first removed from its protective wrapper, it will feel more plastic and must be warmed and conditioned in your hands for several seconds. It will soften quickly but should be warmed thoroughly before using.

The advantages of using Slow Dry Type are its obvious extended working time. This means you can create small, delicate pieces without the edges cracking as quickly due to air drying. Flower petals, stems, etc., can be formed and joined easily. Most exciting of all, Slow Dry Type allows you the time to extrude the clay through an empty syringe into long ropes or strips which then can be woven, braided, or otherwise manipulated without cracking. To be sure, you still need to moisten your work with a damp paintbrush, but you will have an obvious advantage in the length of time you can handle the clay before cracks appear. Remember, however, that if you have five times longer to work with the clay, you also need five times longer to dry the clay.

Art Clay Oil Paste

Art Clay Oil Paste is oil-based. It comes in two separately sealed containers. One has 10gms of the very thick paste, the other contains a thinner that is used to keep the paste at working consistency. Both jars must be kept tightly sealed as they emit a pungent petroleum odor. Also, the thinner will evaporate if left exposed to the air.

Oil Paste has been formulated to act as a bond between *fired silver pieces.* Since fired silver has already attained its maximum shrinkage and the organic binders have already burned out, Oil Paste has an advantage over water-based paste in that it will bind the pieces together beyond the temperature at which the normal clay binders would burn out. It provides a solid weld between pure silver findings, or between two fired silver pieces. In addition, it is highly successful in filling cracks and pits that may have occurred during the initial firing. There are some important tips in using Art Clay Oil Paste:

- Oil Paste must be fired at a lower temperature than regular Art Clay. Fire at 1560°F for 10 minutes, or 1472°F for 30 minutes.
- Oil Paste must be dried completely before firing. That means at least 30 minutes with a hot air drier, or at least 24 hours in room air.
- Oil paste shrinks at the rate typical for all Art Clay products—9 percent to 10 percent. Therefore, be sure to *overfill* when repairing cracks or pits, or removing seams in bezel wire. Excess fired silver can be filed and sanded smooth after firing.

Art Clay Paper Type

Now, for something *completely different!* Aida Chemical Industries created Paper Type for Origami artists. It is a 75mm square sheet, 10gm of clay with nearly all of the water removed. It looks and feels like vinyl, and has tremendous memory. That means when you crease or fold it, it stays that way. Paper Type fires to 99.9 percent fine silver, just like all Art Clay Silver products. But, because it is formulated differently, it does not tolerate additional moisture and you don't have to dry it before firing. There are other unique features:

- Art Clay Paper Type needs to be fired at the lower temperature of 1472°F.
- You must put Paper Type into a cool kiln, below 300°F and take longer than 15 minutes to reach firing temperature.
- You should add pieces and repair cracks with Oil Paste prior to firing, rather than Regular Paste Type.
- If you add excess moisture, Paper Type will lose its shine and begin to degrade.
- The unique consistency of Paper Type makes it perfect to use with paper punches and fancy-edged scissors in creating silver appliqué shapes. These cut outs can be added to dried Art Clay Silver pieces with a very thin layer of regular paste. After air drying and firing, Paper Type can be polished just the same as other Art Clay Silver types.

Art Clay Lowfire Silver Overlay Paste

Silver Overlay Paste is a perfect addition to high-fire glazed porcelain or glass. If you have ever tried using regular Art Clay Silver Types with glazed porcelain, you know that success has been based more on the silver clay's ability to stick to itself, than to the porcelain. There has been more success using Art Clay on bisque, or unglazed porcelain because the rough surface of the ceramic allows the Art Clay to attach more readily. Even the ceramic pieces that you find in the "paint-it-yourself" shops and ceramics stores typically have 06 glazes, which means that the 1600°F firing temperature of Art Clay Silver isn't quite high enough to guarantee a permanent bond. (For a chart of cone firing temperatures, see Appendix, page 128.)

High-fire porcelain, however, is another story. The glazes used on porcelain are of a totally different formulation. They fire at a temperature in excess of 2000°F, are hard, and non-porous. In order for metal clay to consistently bond with these glazes, we have had to rely on the contraction of the silver around the porcelain. Success rates when placing Syringe Type or Clay Type flat onto the porcelain were iffy at best.

Silver Overlay Paste was introduced in the summer of 2002. It was specifically formulated to bond to highfire glazes on porcelain. It is also water based and first came in a 10gm package. In the spring of 2003, it was reformulated to fire at 650°C. or 1200°F, and the bottle size was increased to 15gm. SOL Paste can be used in a variety of ways:

- Painted directly, full strength, onto the bisque, glazed porcelain or glass piece.
- Used in a technique called sgraffito, whereby a thin layer of Overlay Paste is applied to the glazed porcelain or glass, allowed to dry, and a pointed instrument is used to scratch a design into the layer. This allows the porcelain or glass beneath to come through. It is similar to stenciling.
- It can also be used as an alternative to Oil Paste when filling cracks, as well as firing metal to metal.

Six-Fifty Overlay Paste is fired the same as Art Clay Silver 650 Low Fire Clay. You can fire it as low as 1200°F, but it can also be fired at higher temperatures for five minutes.

Art Clay 650 (Lowfire 1200°F)

This type is the most recent addition to the Art Clay Silver family—and is the most exciting and versatile. As with every Art Clay Silver product, it has the same post-firing silver content of 99.9% fine silver. It is packaged in a reusable plastic pouch in the familiar sizes of 10gm, 20gm, and 50gm. It is also available in a Paste Type and a Syringe Type. There are unique distinctions and several major advantages to Art Clay 650's lower firing temperature:

- Art Clay 650 shrinks only 8 percent to 9 percent, a bit less than all the other Art Clay Silver products. This is due to its higher concentration of silver particles.
- It can be fired successfully with sterling silver.
- It can be fired with glass without the distinctive yellowing that typically occurs.
- Glass fired with ACS650 will not slump or flow.
- Some gemstones that were too sensitive or soft to be fired with Art Clay Silver Regular or Slow Dry can be fired with ACS650. These include moonstone, garnets, hematite, obsidian, and diopside.

Firing Art Clay Silver with Other Materials

Gemstones—Heat Versus the Mohs Scale of Hardness

My own personal feeling is that Mr. Mohs had way too much time on his hands. He created a comparative scale of hardness for hundreds of gemstones, using the hardest known to man (diamond) as 10, and the softest (gypsum) as 1. All other stones fall between. For the purposes of our discussion, I'm referring to faceted and unfaceted stones of commercial value. Examples are the so-called "precious" stones of ruby, sapphire (both are chemically in the family corundum), and emerald, semi-precious stones like aquamarine, garnet, and the quartz family (citrine and amethyst), and the popular, softer stones like turquoise.

ACS650 Overlay Paste is water soluble, just like most other ACS products.

Re-closable packages keep the clay moist after opening.

Yellow packaging distinguishes the 650 series.

The general rule-of-thumb states that any stone with a Mohs hardness of 7.5 and above is capable of being fired with Art Clay Silver. However, which stones actually can be fired with Art Clay Regular and Slow Dry depend not only on the hardness of the stone, but its sensitivity to heat. For example, topaz is a fairly common gemstone known for its variety of blues and other colors. It ranks "8" on the Mohs scale. You'd think that it would be safe to fire. After all, controlled heat is used to *enhance* the colors in the majority of topaz stones available in the United States. Unfortunately, that's not the case. Most topaz will lose color during firing. Blues may fade or disappear altogether. They may become dusky and brownish. However, there has been a new "heat diffusion" procedure introduced for topaz, which produces an incredible green that is heat tolerant and permanent. These have been fired successfully with Art Clay Silver.

On a more bizarre note, it's been found that *hardest* doesn't necessarily mean *toughest*. Diamonds cannot be fired in metal clays, though diamonds without major flaws are traditionally left in place during re-tipping and repair. It appears that the prolonged heating necessary to sinter Art Clay Silver has a negative effect on the diamond and may reduce it to its original constituents—carbon ash. Not a pleasant result for such a valuable stone. Personally, diamonds have never much appealed to me, and there are far more colorful and naturally valuable gemstones to use in Art Clay.

Refer to appendix (page 128) for a list of the most common stones and their ranking on the Mohs scale as well as their ability to fire in Art Clay Silver Clay Types.

Laboratory Created Stones Versus Synthetic Stones

Here's where terms become vague and fairly subjective. I had always been told that the term "synthetic stone" referred to any stone that was not natural. That meant those stones formed from plastic or resin, glass, or laboratory-created stones. Lately, I've heard differing definitions. You may or may not agree with my definitions. However, the most important thing you should remember is to ask questions. If the word "synthetic" is used in reference to any stone you purchase, my advice is **not** to place the stone into your piece until you've gotten more information about its origin, or tested it yourself.

I prefer to separate stones into three groups: natural, lab created, and synthetic.
- NATURAL—this should refer to any stones dug out of the earth, i.e. ruby, sapphire, emerald, jasper, turquoise, etc. These may or may not be able to be fired in a kiln or with a torch. Many natural stones have inclusions, cracks, or other imperfections that weaken them or put them at risk of fracturing when fired.
- LAB CREATED—these are stones that are chemically identical to those natural stones above, but have been man-made in a laboratory using pressure and heat or irradiation to "fast-forward" Nature's natural process. Lab-created stones are generally cheaper than natural stones, but they have the advantage of purity, which most naturally created stones lack. This purity makes them more stable during the firing process. Examples include lab-created ruby, sapphire, and tanzanite. One of the most recognizable, the Chatham emerald, is lab-created.
- SYNTHETIC—stones that are called synthetic can be made of anything. They can be lab-created, but they can also be doublets: a base of natural stone that is topped by a clear or colored cap of quartz, glass, or plastic. The most common faceted gemstone doublets sold are garnet, sapphire, and emerald, just to name a few. The problem is that, unless you have experience, doublets are very difficult to identify with the naked eye or even a jeweler's loupe. When fired, the doublet top may melt, cloud or change color.

ACS 650 Lowfire clay was used to add the starfish and dolphin to this sterling wire. It was then fired at 1250°F for 30 minutes.

Brass wire imbedded into ACS Regular. Filing and polishing achieved the finish. The Liver of Sulfur was used to turn the silver into a hematite-like black.

Jasper and agate river rocks.

Natural Stones—River Rocks and Ugly Stones

The difference between these "natural stones" and others is that the natural stones are not faceted or finished in any way beyond tumbling to a rough polish. River stones are large pebbles made smooth by eons of water coursing over them. Rough nuggets of granite, jasper, and agate are in this category. The only way to assure that they will survive firing is to pre-fire them in your kiln at 1472°F for 30 minutes or, if using them with ACS 650, at 1200°F for 30 minutes. Wrap them in fiber blanket or similar material so if they burst or explode during firing they won't damage your kiln.

Wire and Other Metals—Silver and Nickel and Brass, Oh My!

Since Art Clay Silver is 99.9 percent fine, it is logical and pretty obvious that fine silver wire will fire successfully with all types of Art Clay. Sterling, on the other hand, which is only 92.5 percent silver, has a lower melting point than pure silver and is not recommended for firing with Art Clay Silver Regular and Slow Dry types. In addition, the non-silver alloys, which include nickel and copper, react badly with the heat. Not only do they become an ugly black, but sterling weakens during firing. It is possible to sand or file away the black color, but the weakened condition of the wire may cause it to break or crack. I've tried firing sterling ear posts at 1472°F and though they polished up with some effort, they soon broke off at the base.

Art Clay Silver 650 is the perfect solution. Sterling silver very easily survives the firing temperature of 1250°F and can be used with confidence. Don't forget, however, that the firing process will anneal the wire and it must be hardened by placing the piece on a mandrel or bench pin and tapping with a rawhide mallet until sufficiently rigid, or reheating the piece to 600°F for 40-50 minutes.

Brass alloy, which is comprised of copper and zinc, is another possible addition to Art Clay Silver. I've often pressed brass mesh into a ball of Art Clay Silver and fired the two

Dichroic glass cabochon and Art Clay Silver regular fired at 1472°F for 30 minutes.

together. The brass survives and the pattern created is unique and pleasing, especially when the Liver of Sulfur is used as a patina. Imbedding brass wire into Art Clay Silver has been a part of our advanced curriculum since the beginning, and it remains one of my favorite techniques. The contrast of the bright yellow brass against the hematite appearance of patinaed silver is extraordinary. We've included a project using brass mesh in this book.

Bronze, on the other hand, is a no-no. Though there are various formulae for this alloy, lead and/or aluminum may be included, and the presence of either will ruin your piece.

Glass and Art Clay—Going with the Flow

There are few things as compatible with Art Clay Silver as glass. And few things as complex. The physics of fusing glass is a chapter unto itself, and will be discussed more fully later in this book. For the moment, suffice it to say that fused glass and fired Art Clay Silver are similar in that both are a result of time and temperature. You can fire either one at a lower temperature for a longer time, or a higher temperature for a shorter time. When using Slow Dry or Regular Art Clay this is a very desirable relationship. The temperatures at which most brands of glass fully fuse fall between the sintering temperatures for Art Clay Silver—1472°F and 1600°F. If you know how the glass will behave at those temperatures, you will have no trouble combining the two, with incredible results.

Glass and Art Clay overlay.

Firing glass with Art Clay Silver 650 clay or overlay paste is even easier. Because the sintering temperature of 1200°F falls below the fusing and slumping temperature of most glass, the only thing you need to be concerned about is annealing. Again, we'll cover that in Chapter 2. I must say, however, that though using glass with ACS 650 is easier and requires less knowledge of hot glass, I prefer to fire my glass and Art Clay at the higher temperatures. I like my glass to flow and "become one" with the silver, not just be an extension of it.

Faux raku is an easy effect to create with Art Clay Silver Paste Type, a terra cotta pot, and Liver of Sulfur.

Ceramics—Other Clays that Crack Me Up

It used to be a whole lot easier. You had ceramics, such as stoneware, terra cotta and other pottery clays. You had Art Clay Silver Regular or Slow Dry. You put the Art Clay around the glazed or unglazed bisque ceramic piece, heated it slowly so the ceramics wouldn't crack from thermal shock, brought it to the necessary sintering temperature, and then cooled it slowly. There wasn't too much else to say. Except for porcelain. High fire, hard glazes, and harder bisque thwarted most attempts to bond Art Clay to it. You could encircle the porcelain with the silver clay and use the shrinkage factor to keep it attached after firing. But more complex unions were often unsuccessful.

Enter Art Clay Silver 650 Overlay Paste. It looks a lot like Oil Paste, except that it's water soluble. And it fires onto glazed porcelain. It doesn't just "fire" onto it, it *bonds* with it, permanently. Art Clay SOL Paste fires more easily than any of the other clays or pastes. Pieces are brought to at least 1200°F degrees and the temperature held for 30 minutes. You let the porcelain cool to under 300°F and then remove the piece from the kiln. And, we're not talking just porcelain cabochons here. We're talking porcelain cups, saucers, picture frames, spoons, mementoes, broken shards of vases and those same cups and saucers. Porcelain beads are terrific! Art Clay has a separate book dedicated to the Overlay Paste technique, but we'll have a project included in this book as well, just to whet your appetite. It's truly amazing stuff, and extremely easy to use.

And let's not forget ceramic pots and vases. One of my favorite affects is what I call a "faux" raku. You take an unglazed, terra cotta pot of some kind (smaller is cheaper) and you paint two to three layers of Art Clay Silver Paste over the outside, letting each dry between layers. Then you fire the pot according to the appropriate instructions. After you brush the silver veneer to a matte silver finish, you sand it lightly, wash with baking soda and water, and dip in hot Liver of Sulfur to achieve a rainbow of raku-like colors: an absolutely extraordinary affect. We'll be going over the use of Liver of Sulfur in detail later. Once you get the hang of using it, the beautiful colors will be well worth the terrible stink!

Tools of the Trade

What You Absolutely Have to Have

The beauty of using Art Clay Silver is that there *aren't* a lot of tools needed. No fancy mechanical, electrical, high priced melting, squeezing, or pressing things. The essentials are found around the house or at a local craft/hobby store without too much fuss.

1. **Some kind of rolling thing**—this can be as simple as a 4-6" piece of 1" PVC tubing, or the nice, acrylic rolling pin Art Clay World sells.

Acrylic roller.

2. **Measuring levels**—can be made out of cardboard, plastic, or playing cards taped together. You need two, each at least 1.2mm thick, to put on either side of the clay so that when you roll it out, you roll it on the levels. This creates a consistent, minimum thickness recommended for your piece. The absolute thinnest Art Clay World recommends is 1mm. With anything thinner than that, your piece won't be structurally strong enough after firing.

1mm plastic strips.

3. **A pointed and/or flat-end paintbrush**—used to dampen your wet clay to keep it moist, apply Paste Type between two pieces, and a myriad of other little jobs. We recommend the white Taklon bristles, though you can use anything that doesn't hold the clay and turn the tip into a big blob.

Paintbrush.

4. **Something to keep your leftover Art Clay in**—again, this can be anything from plastic wrap, to a recloseable bag, to a screw-top jar that will keep air out and the moisture in. Art Clay World, USA, has one we call a Clay Keeper.

Clay Keeper, 4 oz.

5. **A work surface**—even if you only use room air to dry your pieces, you need to have a non-porous place to roll out your clay. Something the silver clay won't stick to after it's dry. In the past, people have used parchment or baking sheet, rigid acrylic and glass surfaces, marble or ceramic tiles. Personally, I swear by the Teflon-coated work surfaces that we have now. They're flexible, easy to transport to the drier if you wish and, best of all, are totally non-stick. Once your piece has begun to dry, the Teflon-coated sheet releases it, allowing you to flip the piece over, and remove it undisturbed; it prevents cracking or breakage.

Teflon-coated work surface. Art Clay pieces will slide off when dried.

6" flexible tissue blade with safety case.

6. **A craft knife, short or long**—whether the typical X-acto or Excel type, short bladed stencil knife, or long, 6" flexible blade, you'll need something for cutting clay and other things.

7. **A container with clean water**—plastic cup, glass, even old film canisters. You'll need just enough water to keep your brushes clean and deep enough to rest your open syringe tip-down, so it doesn't dry out.

Art Clay World recommends 3 grits of sandpaper: 600, 1200 and 2000.

8. **Files or sandpaper**—I suppose your mom's old pumice stone would work in a pinch, but you'll want to remove unwanted clay and smooth your piece prior to firing. And, unless you're a forger for some unscrupulous archeologist, you'll want your pieces to look better than those dug up at Pompeii. Just an assumption.

9. **Some kind of oil or petroleum-based lubrication for your hands and tools**—I love olive oil. Extra virgin, if possible, but not mandatory. I much prefer olive oil on my hands to Badger Balm, Udder Balm, Bag Balm, whatever those other moisturizing lotions are. I don't like the stickiness of them. Olive oil is natural, doesn't smell (other than of Nana's salad!) and works right into your skin. You only want to apply the barest touch. Enough to keep the silver clay from sticking to your hands and your roller. NEVER over-lubricate your hands! Too much oil on your hands will work itself into the Art Clay and you'll wind up with something akin to crumbly piecrust dough.

10. **Wooden mandrel**—if you ever plan on making rings, and 95 percent of Art Clay Silver users do, you'll need some kind of tapering wooden mandrel. It does really have to be wood, not metal, for a number of reasons.

Wooden mandrel.

- Wood doesn't conduct heat. If you're using a hot air drier of some kind, you're likely to burn your fingers touching a metal mandrel.
- A metal mandrel will also expand to a small degree when heated. That will make your ring seem too loose, or allow it to contract too much during drying, which will change the finished size of your ring.

Stovetop firing programmable kiln, or butane torch. Each will achieve the desired results.

11. **Something to Sinter the clay**—a gas stovetop, butane torch, or electric kiln (programmable strongly suggested). Whichever you choose, the main function is to heat the dried silver clay to sintering temperature and hold it there until the process is complete and the organic binders and water have burned off. Each method has its pros and cons, whether it's expense, or size limitations. In the chapter on firing, we'll go over each and give you the information you need to decide objectively which procedure is best for your circumstances.

Regular hairdryers are cheap and convenient, but they have their own limitations.

Three-stage magnifying visor.

What Will Make Your Life a Whole Lot Easier

There are some things that aren't essential, merely convenient. You *could* do without them—but who'd want to?

- A **hot air dryer** of some kind—the most often used is a hairdryer. There are other, better ways to dry your clay, but we'll go into that in more detail later. Bottom line, they dry the clay in a fraction of the time it takes to air dry it. So, if you don't have all the time in the world, this item crosses the line from "want to have" to "must have."

- **Clay shaping tools**—there are all sorts, made out of wood, rubber, silicone. They push, gouge, scrape, and shape your wet clay. Again, a toothpick might work, but real tools just aren't that expensive and offer a whole level of ease and efficiency you just can't beat.

Cleaning tool.

- A **magnifier**—this is one of those "line crossing" items. Personally, I can't see well enough to work *without* a magnifier these days, but even if I could, I'd want to use one. There are defects you can see in pre-fired clay pieces with a magnifier that you just wouldn't notice with your bare eyes. My philosophy: if it passes my inspection while I'm wearing a magnifier, then it will certainly pass an "eye clean" inspection by any of my students, teachers, or customers.

- A **wooden mandrel** with a metal stand—once you've used one of these, you'll never go back to balancing a regular mandrel on your lap again. Made by DuMatt Company, this increasingly popular metal stand is in the shape of an "L" and has a pin that comes out on which you place the accompanying mandrel (which has a matching hole drilled in the thick end). This frees your hands to work with the clay, steadies the mandrel, and allows you to rotate it when adding designs, decorations, or just fine-tuning your ring. It is absolutely, positively worth the money, and sits ever-so-nicely under your hot-air-whatever.

Wooden mandrel with a removable metal stand.

I'm sure you can think of other tools, gizmos, and frufrus that would make your Art Clay experience faster, easier, and more pleasant. Art Clay instructors and users are calling all the time with suggestions and new tools or tips they've discovered. Some are mentioned in this book, others have become creative secrets. No doubt you'll come up with a few of your own.

Chapter Two

The Process

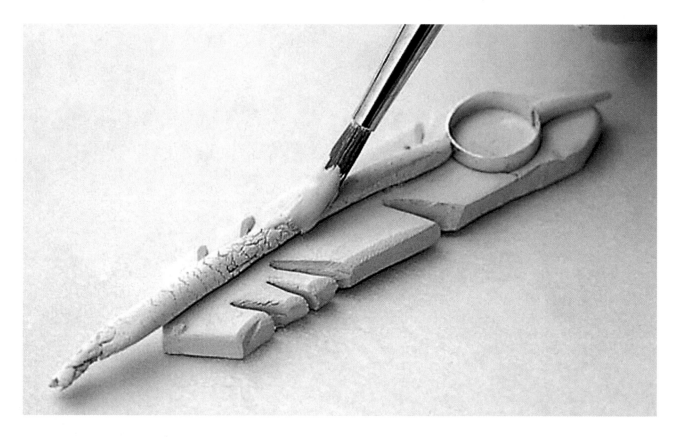

The actual act of creating a finished piece of Art Clay Silver requires completing three stages: the wet stage, the greenware stage, and the fired stage. Each is a unique and distinct component of the creative process, and each has its own techniques and challenges.

The secret to success in working with Art Clay Silver is to spend 10 percent of the time working in the wet stage, 80 percent in the greenware stage, and 10 percent in the fired stage. Of course, it would be ludicrous to take this statement literally, but my point is that spending too much time in the wet stage will create all kinds of difficulties for you, not the least of which is the losing battle with air. And, having to spend a great deal of time polishing the piece after it's fired is a waste of your valuable time. While the Art Clay Silver is wet, you can do all the preliminary steps: shape, cut, mold, and sculpt. But get those preliminaries out of the way. The sooner your piece dries, the better. Why? Because your time in the wet state is limited. The amount of time you can spend in the dried greenware state, however, is *un*limited. Once the Art Clay Silver is dried in its basic shape, you have all the time in the world to fine tune it. There is no such thing as *too* dry. And filing and sanding in a greenware state is much, much easier than in a hard, silver state. Not to mention that, before firing, all the filings, sanding dust, bits, and pieces can be reconstituted with water into paste that can be used for all kinds of things.

A bit about preplanning: Your need for the precautions mentioned will be reduced if you give some thought as to what you are going to need for any particular Art Clay project. There is nothing worse than rolling out your clay and realizing you don't have your paintbrushes, water, or other tools handy. If you're going to be making a pendant, you need to think about how you are going to hang it. Are you going to create the bail out of Art Clay, use a jump ring through a hole in the piece, add a pure silver bailback or a screweye? Will you need a straw, toothpick, or bamboo skewer? Do you have your olive oil for your hands and tools? The better prepared you are, the more time you will actually have to create your piece. That's one of the reasons Art Clay World, USA created the Tool Kit; it keeps everything you need in one place.

Use slats to roll your clay to keep the thickness consistent.

Stage One— Forming in the Wet State

You've opened the package—and, once Art Clay Silver is exposed to the air, the clay will begin to dry. Even the Slow Dry Type is susceptible, though it dries five times more slowly. In order to shape, mold, and sculpt, keeping the clay moist is of the utmost importance. One of the best ways to do this is to plan ahead. Here are some of the ways you can keep Art Clay moist while working with it:

- Use a re-sealable bag.
- Cover your extra clay and in-progress work with plastic wrap.
- Place extra clay loosely between layers of damp paper toweling.
- Get a small, screw-top jar, like Art Clay's "Clay keeper," that has a compartment for your damp sponge.
- Have a humidifier/mister at your workstation.

Paint leaves with Paste Type.

I'm sure there are other ways people manage this challenge, but one will generally work for you.

Workin' It
In the wet stage, Art Clay can be used in many ways. The Regular clay type can be rolled over smooth or textured surfaces, and rolled into ropes and snakes. You can roll lace and textured objects into the Art Clay, or press the clay into a pre-made mold. Additionally, Slow Dry and Art Clay 650 types can be extruded through an empty syringe into long ropes, which then can be braided.

Paste Type can be painted in layers over any range of organic forms, such as leaves, pods, twigs, paper, cork clay … in fact, anything that can burn out in a kiln at the sintering temperatures. It can be used as a "glue" to join two or more unfired clay pieces together, or used to add findings to unfired clay pieces.

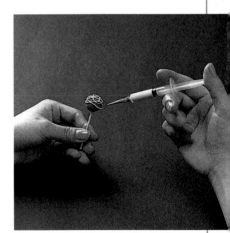

Syringe Type on this ball of cork clay will become a hollow silver ball.

Syringe Type can be used to create a beaded border, filigree, dots, and coils. Use it to fill cracks in clay before firing or adding findings to unfired clay.

How's It Hangin?
Once you've got the initial form of your piece, if its intended use is body adornment, you need to create a way to wear it.

When creating holes, remember two things— don't use a straw with a small opening. After the piece is fired, it may be too small to fit a jump ring. Secondly, watch where you put the hole. Too close to the top and the thin area might crack when fired. To far from the top and you won't be able to attach the jump ring, or it won't be able to function.

The simplest form of hanging is to create a hole in the clay and, after it's fired, to insert a jump ring(s) and a chain. If the ACS is still wet, making the hole is a snap. Get a drinking straw and press firmly into the clay. You can blow the little piece left in the straw out, or pick it out of the clay if it's still in the clay. It is *not* suggested that you just use a toothpick or other solid object to create the hole. Why not? Because not only will you create a hole, you'll also create a messy bunch of ridges and bumps around it caused by the displaced clay. Then you'll have more cleanup. Using some form of straw is much cleaner, neater, and faster.

A "rollover" bail is actually part of the piece itself. It's created by extending the top of the clay when you roll it out. Then you place some kind of mandrel or spacer on the clay and roll the clay over it, attaching the clay to itself on the other side. The mandrel can consist of a wooden toothpick, bamboo skewer, paper straw, or even a small twig. Any of these can remain in the piece and will burn out in the kiln. ***Important warning***: Do not use any plastic straws, plastic foam shapes, or other plastic-based forms if you plan to leave them in. Burning plastic in any form will result in the release of toxic fumes that are harmful to your lungs. If you **must** use a plastic straw, lubricate it first with olive oil and, when the piece is dried, remove the straw before firing.

Pure Silver Findings are made for Art Clay World specifically for use with Art Clay. They are in whole, or part 99.9 percent pure silver and can be fired in with the Art Clay piece at the normal firing temperatures. There are three basic kinds of pure silver findings that relate to wearability. These are the bailback, the brooch finding, and the flat screw eye. The bailback is an "ear-" shaped finding that can be attached to the back of a piece of greenware using Paste or Syringe Type clay. It has the benefit of having an invisible profile, meaning you can't see the finding from the front of the finished piece.

The brooch pin comes in three or four parts (depending on the model). Two of the parts are pure silver and are attached to the back of a greenware piece, much the same as the bailback. After firing, the non-silver pieces (which include the actual pin) are reattached and the piece is ready to use. This virtually eliminates the need to glue or solder your brooch findings to your pieces. For me, who hates to use any kind of glue, this is a *big* deal!

Choosing the right sized straw is important.

The flat screw eye is a straight piece of silver with a round "eye" at one end. It is inserted into wet clay at the spot from where you would like the piece to hang. Done properly, only the eye shows. After firing, you would insert a jump ring or snap-on bail to complete the piece. Note: Screw eyes can also be used as connectors or attachments for beads or pearls.

Adding Stuff

There are two basic ways of adding faceted gemstones to your Art Clay Silver piece. For those gemstones that you can fire in Art Clay Regular, Slow Dry, or 650/1200, the process involves either pushing the stone into the wet clay, or creating a "seat" for the stone out of coiled Syringe Type Clay. Either way, it is vital that the girdle of the stone (the widest diameter) be imbedded and covered by clay. If not, when the piece is fired and the clay shrinks, instead of locking the stone in, it will push the stone up and out. When done properly, your stone will be locked permanently in place and will look like it was bezel-set.

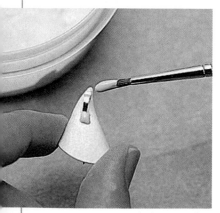

Use Paste Type to attach this pure silver ball back to eliminates the need to solder.

To successfully set stones into the clay, here are some important tips:

- When possible, use a straw or punch to create a small hole in the clay that is smaller than the stone. This will allow the culet (the bottommost point) of the faceted stone to hang suspended into the hole. The surrounding clay will protect it, but light will be permitted to travel inside and through the stone unimpeded.

- Place the stone on a flat surface upside down, resting on the table of the stone. Use a tweezers or similar tool to pick up the stone and carefully turn the tweezers so it is right side up. Drop the stone into the hole prepared in the clay.

- Hold the entire piece at eye level and press on the table of the stone in the center. This will ensure that the stone is set level into the clay. Continue to look at the setting from several directions to make certain the table is level. Make adjustments as needed and dry.

- After the piece is dry, make sure the girdle is totally imbedded in the clay.

- Clean the table and upper facets of extraneous paste/clay types so that only the very endmost edge of the girdle is covered. Do not cover the main facets with clay. This will make the stone appear smaller and diminish the play of light on the stone. More importantly, if any silver clay or paste is left on the stone when it is fired, it will fume onto the stone, discoloring it (this is true for glass as well).

- Do NOT clean the stone when the clay is wet. This will just smear the clay and put a finer coating of clay on the stone. Wait until the piece is dry, and gently brush the surface of the stone until it is clean.

For faceted stones you cannot fire in place, it is possible to use a pure silver, calibrated setting prior to firing. These settings are available in various sizes and shapes. They can be placed into the clay while it is wet, or added with paste after initial drying. Once fired, any stone that fits the setting can be dropped into place and the prongs tightened by using a jeweler's pliers on opposing prongs and gently squeezing until they are pressing tightly against the stone. Tapping on the stone with the tip of a pair of pliers will tell you whether it is tight. If it moves, repeat the process.

Examples of natural and stones en cabochon are natural river rock, and what are commonly referred to as "cabs." *En cabochon* is a French term referring strictly to the **shape** of the polished stone: flat on the bottom and domed or a flattened round top. Cabs can be freeform or calibrated to specific, most commonly sought-after shapes and sizes. Examples are ovals, round, emerald or octagon, pear and marquis or navette. Sizes are typically in millimeters, such as 6mm x 4mm, 7mm x 5mm, 18mm x 24mm, etc. There are numerous size charts available through jewelry company catalogs, and on-line. Nearly none of the natural and cabbed stones typically used with Art Clay can be fired in place. Exceptions are natural or lab created ruby and emerald crystals, and precious stones that have been cabbed instead of faceted (usually because of lesser quality rough material). Other examples of commonly cabbed stones include malachite, turquoise, agates, jaspers, and opals. All of these stones are either too soft or too fragile to withstand the high firing temperatures.

TIP:

When deciding what to use as your mandrel, think of how large your chain and clasp will be. Creating a beautiful rollover bail that doesn't permit the chain to go through isn't very functional. I've actually started my own collection of large diameter straws garnered from jumbo shake places. It was a sacrifice, but someone had to do it!

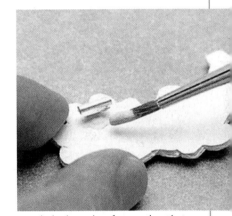

Attach the brooch safety catch with Art Clay and fire it on.

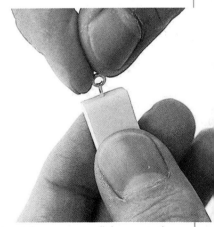

Insert the screw-eye all the way to the eye prior to drying.

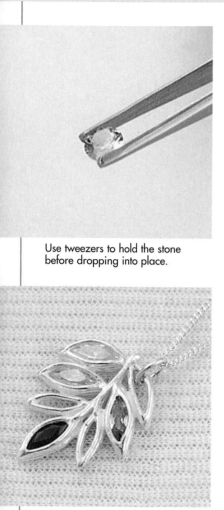

Use tweezers to hold the stone before dropping into place.

Lab created sapphire set into a syringe-created pendant. This is a Level I certification project.

When using these stones, a setting must be created to hold them in place; one that can be fired prior to the stone being set. The most common setting is called a bezel setting. Instead of using prongs to capture the girdle of the faceted stone, the bezel setting consists of a thin, flat strip of metal (called a flat bezel wire) that encircles the stone and is manually pushed against it to hold it in place with a bezel pusher or a bezel setter. When using Art Clay Silver, this wire is attached to the body of the piece by pressing slightly into the wet clay, sealing with Paste Type, drying and firing. During the sintering process, the clay will shrink slightly but the pure silver bezel wire will not. This will cause the clay to "lock" the bezel in place. There may or may not be a slight concavity that forms, but this can be easily tapped out with a rawhide mallet. After the piece is cooled and polished, the stone is dropped into the setting and the bezel wire closed around the stone.

Some helpful tips for working with Art Clay and bezel settings:

- After measuring the wire around the stone, use a file to create flat, straight edges that meet well and evenly together.

- Before placing the bezel wire around the stone, flatten the piece of wire and draw a very fine line, approximately $1/32$" from the edge of the wire with a marker. This will help you bury the flat wire evenly into the clay and avoid high and low spots.

- Use Oil Paste or Silver Overlay Paste on the seam instead of solder. Dry and fire just the bezel. File and sand until the seam has disappeared.

- If you have a shallow stone, or have used an overly wide bezel wire, you can raise the level of the stone so that the bezel doesn't crease when you close it, or cover too much of the cabochon. This is done by placing a layer of another material inside the bezel. Materials that work include cardboard, sawdust (both of which will deteriorate with time), a thin layer of metal, and our choice, fiber paper. The fiber paper is a compressed ceramic fiber so that even if it gets wet, it will dry out and last a relatively long time. Also it is so thin that several layers can be used as needed.

For another method of holding cabochons in place, create your own prongs by folding small pieces of 18 or 20 gauge wire tightly in half and bury the raw ends into the clay around the perimeter of the stone. Remove the stone, use Paste Type to reinforce the wire and dry. After firing and polishing, replace the stone and very carefully bend the wires to capture the stone. You can even use Syringe Type to decorate the wires. The secret to success here is to bend very slowly and not torque or twist the wires.

With the addition of Art Clay 650 Low Fire & Silver Overlay Paste, there are now three methods of adding glass to Art Clay Silver.

Regular and Slow Dry clays shrink 9 percent to 10 percent, but the more significant issue is heat. The physics of hot glass has filled many, many books, and understanding what happens to glass when it is heated is essential to successfully combining it with metal clay.

Glass goes through several stages while heating and each is important. The first stage is when you put glass in the kiln and begin heating it. If you heat a piece of thick glass too quickly, it will thermal shock and crack or break. To avoid this, you need to slow the speed at which you "ramp" up your kiln, or heat it. What is too thick? Over one-quarter inch in thickness and larger than a silver dollar. That means, thankfully, that the small glass cabochons we frequently fire with Art Clay are relatively safe to fire in the kiln without too much worry about thermal shock.

The next stage is the Transition stage, when the glass is going from a solid to a fluid state. This is when glass will slump with gravity, which begins to happen around 1250°F. Above this temperature, glass continues to become softer and softer until, at around 1800°F to 2000°F, it is the consistency of viscous honey. Fusing temperatures, for all intents and purposes, are around 1450°F to 1650°F. Toward the lower end, the glass will flow less readily, toward the upper end, it will flow more readily. However, the most dangerous issue when firing Art Clay with glass is incompatibility. And, to understand the danger and prevent it, we have to talk about co-efficients of expansion, or COE.

"Cabs" are stones with a flat bottom and domed top.

As most of us remember from our schooling, metal generally expands when heated, and contracts when cooled. What you may not remember, is that everything else does as well, if not to the same degree. Glass, ceramics, and metal all expand with heat, and contract when cooled. The *amount* to which they contract is calculated as an exponential number. The exponent is not written, and the remaining number is used as a guide. COEs are routinely used to compare sheets of glass, since each glass company uses a different formula and not all of them are compatible with each other. Therefore, COEs of 90, 96, and 104 are familiar to glass fusers and help them determine which glasses can be fired together. Two pieces of glass that aren't compatible will crack at the point of joining when cooled.

Art Clay has its own COE but, because it is metal-based, we don't need to know its value to know that pure silver will contract more than the glass. In addition, because of the conductive properties of metal, the silver will release heat faster than the glass, causing dangerous stress in the glass as it goes from a fluid state to a solid state.

Pure silver calibrated mountings are perfect for faceted stones that can't be fired in place.

And, if that isn't enough stress, cooling glass will store even more if it can't cool evenly. The process of releasing stress in glass during cooling is called *annealing*. And glass that isn't annealed properly can store enough residual stress to crack hours, days, weeks, even months later. Fortunately, as in the case of thermal shock, most glass that we use in jewelry is small enough to anneal simply by keeping the kiln door closed until close to room temperature.

However, all of these factors need to be taken into consideration when firing metal with glass. We are including a few Art Clay and glass projects later in this book, but here are some tips to help you complete them successfully:

- Allow for the appropriate shrinkage when designing your piece. Wrapping the clay too tightly around the glass prior to firing will result in cracking of your glass and/or clay.

- Before firing your glass and Art Clay, make very sure that you've cleaned the surface of your glass by brushing with a dry brush and, if necessary, alcohol. Any stray silver residue left on the glass will cause it to "fume," yellow, or cloud.

- Unless you are firing your glass with Art Clay 650 Low Fire, you will need to be aware that the heat required to fire the Art Clay will cause your glass to "move" or flow. If planned, this can be a terrific design element. If not, it can be a huge disappointment.

NOTE:

It is strongly suggested that you use a magnifier, either tabletop or headset variety, when working with gemstones and other finely detailed techniques. My general rule-of-thumb is, if I am satisfied with the result at magnification, then the average person will find it acceptable, or "eye clean" in normal light.

- Art Clay Silver (in fact, any silver) will cause clear glass to develop yellow or brown stains when fired together at the sintering temperature of 1472°F or higher. To avoid this, protect the clear glass with a black marker (which will burn off during sintering), use dark glass and/or dichroic coatings to mask the stain, or, use Art Clay 650/1200 Lowfire. At 1200°F, your glass will not yellow, soften, slump, or move.

- The temperature window for annealing glass is, generally, between 1050°F and 700°F. You want to avoid opening, venting, or otherwise peeping into kilns when cooling glass is within this temperature range. If you MUST remove glass at the very soonest, wait until the kiln's pyrometer reads 500°F or lower and, using a glove rated 1000°F or more, quickly remove the glass with a tong or spatula, and place between two thick layers of fiber blanket to complete the cooling process. This only applies to small, jewelry-sized pieces of glass.

An important note about firing glass with metal clay: One of the myths that has persisted states that you cannot fire metal clay and glass in the same kiln—that, by doing so, you will "contaminate" your glass forever and you should have one kiln for glass and one for metal clay.

My own, personal theory is that this myth started because some metal clay worker either didn't clean his or her glass surface properly prior to firing, or used a loose fiber kiln, such as those constructed from tool boxes. In either situation, silver trapped on the surface of the glass or within the cotton-type fibers of the kiln contaminated the glass and fogged it. And, since we all know that when something goes wrong it's *never* the user's fault, always the product/object/machine's, the problem was blamed on the metal clay.

Before I heard this myth, I had already been firing glass and Art Clay together for nearly two years and had never, honestly, *never* had a single instance of glass fogging or otherwise becoming contaminated. However, I had had years of glass experience prior to adding Art Clay, so was fairly well prepared for the results I got.

I truly feel there are a tremendous number of people who like the look of glass and/or dichroic glass with the metal clay but aren't experienced in either, and haven't taken the time to learn or understand one's effect upon the other. Some may totally underestimate the learning curve involved in order to produce successful results. That means *predictable*, successful results.

Word of advice: Take the time to learn how Art Clay and glass work together. Familiarize yourself with processes like annealing, thermal shock, devitrification, and staining. You'll have much more success and will save yourself invaluable time and disappointment.

Wire

We've already talked about which different kinds of wire can be used with Art Clay. Now's the time to talk about the how and why. Well, the "why" is, presumably, because you *want* to. The "how" will take a little longer to explain, depending on the kind of wire and how you're going to use it with Art Clay.

Pure Silver Wire

There are several methods of including pure silver wire in your pieces:

- As an armature in a bracelet. Wrapping Art Clay over a 12 gauge wire to form a cuff bracelet is described in one of Art Clay's instruction books. The wire adds strength and flexibility to the fired silver.

- As a finding. I often cut a ¼" piece of 18 gauge silver wire and bend it into a horseshoe shape to insert into the wet clay instead of using a flat screw eye. I do this mainly because I feel that having two points of attachment instead of one is inherently stronger.

- As a decorative element. I've taken 28 gauge fine silver wire and crocheted or knitted it, adding it into wet clay as a design element.

- As a point of attachment for a pearl. Whether freshwater or saltwater, pearls often add a touch of class. One of the most common ways to add pearls is to first fire a small piece (½" or so) of 18 or 20 gauge silver wire into the clay. After firing, a half-drilled pearl is fitted onto the wire and glued in place.

Sterling Silver Wire

Sterling 925 (which contains copper) will blacken and become brittle after firing at 1472°F or 1600°F. It has never been recommended for use with Art Clay Regular or Slow Dry. However, with the advent of Art Clay 650/1200 Low Fire, sterling silver can be successfully added without any adverse affects. Gentle rubbing with a fine grit sandpaper will remove any blackening.

Brass Wire

When adding it as a design element, brass will be easier to use and manipulate if it is annealed first to soften it. This is done by placing the wire on a piece of fiberboard and heating to 1472°F for 1-2 minutes. Remove the wire from the heat and allow to cool. Do *not* quench in water, or the wire will immediately harden. Once at room temperature, the annealed wire can be bent and formed into the desired shape. If it becomes too hard to work with, repeat the annealing procedure.

Some tips to successfully include brass wire in Art Clay:

- After your brass wire has been bent into the desired shape, place on a flat surface and tap flat with a rawhide or rubber mallet. If the wire doesn't lay flat on the silver clay when you press it in, you'll be filing it down inconsistently after the Art Clay is fired.

- Before setting into the wet clay, gently file the topmost point of the round wire slightly to flatten it. This will make it easier to expose the brass wire evenly after firing.

- Do not press the brass into the clay more than halfway. If you do, you may find that, on firing, the underside of the piece may crack if there isn't enough clay to cover the brass.

- Make sure you have at least ⅛" of silver clay surrounding your brass wire after it is set into the piece. If not, the silver border might crack on firing.

Pure silver wire folded into prongs and fired into the clay hold this Mawsitsit jade cab in place.

This bezel wire has been fitted around the cab, its ends filed even, and waits to have the seam coated with oil paste and fired.

A beautiful Art Clay pendant.

- Cover the exposed brass with a thick coating of Art Clay Silver paste type, making sure to get into all the edges of the brass. You want to make sure that the silver clay is covering all brass surfaces. I liken this to seeing a deep layer of snow on a log. You can still see the outline of the log, but the wood itself is not exposed. (For those of you in the warm South, use your imagination!)

- Remember to fire your piece at 1472°F for 30 minutes—any higher and the brass wire will degrade and ruin your piece.

- After firing, remember to cover your piece and use a rawhide mallet to tap out any concavity that has occurred due to shrinkage. This will help you greatly when you're filing to expose the brass wire.

- When filing the fired silver away to reveal the brass, be sure to file only *toward* the wire. Filing away from the wire may pull the silver out of the piece and create pits or cracks that will have to be repaired. Also, file in long, slow, controlled strokes. This will allow you to see your progress and prevent over-filing.

- Do NOT use Wenol as a final polishing element *before* using Liver of Sulfur to create a hematite finish. Wenol leaves a protective coating that will interfere with the Liver of Sulfur patina; after rinsing thoroughly following the use of patina, buff with a clean cloth until the appropriate shine appears.

Ceramics

We're going to talk about the two basic varieties of ceramics and how to use Art Clay with each.

Unglazed Ceramics (Bisqueware)
Unfired ceramics are those with cone firings of 06, and includes terra cotta, the traditional ceramic ware, and those ceramics found in the "paint-it-yourself" stores. It does *not* apply to high-fire porcelain, whether glazed or unglazed.

In the past, ceramics have had to be in the bisque state to achieve any success when adding Art Clay Silver. This has been because Art Clay has needed the rough surface of the ceramics to attach to during firing. Even with the relatively Lowfire, 06 glazes, Art Clay would have difficulties bonding to the glazed surface and would sometimes flake off after cooling. You'll get the best success if you apply Paste Type to unglazed ceramic beads in multiple coats.

Tips when using Art Clay Silver with ceramic bisqueware:

- Clean the ceramics thoroughly with alcohol and let dry. This removes any oils or dirt that would impede attachment.

- In the case of beads, coat the bead thoroughly, inside and out, if possible. Apply at least two, and preferably three coats, of Silver Paste.

- Fire slowly (suggested ramp speed of 1500°F per hour), to avoid cracking the ceramics. Thick or heavy pieces may need to be heated even more slowly.

On the bisque, success has been general, but not guaranteed. I created this Egyptian masque by using regular Syringe and Clay Types, attaching them directly to the bisque. While you can see that the majority of the fired silver has attached well, what you don't see is a "beauty mark" that I had created with Syringe Type to her cheek. Following firing, that small dot of Art Clay flaked right off, perhaps not being large enough to "grab" onto the surface of the porcelain.

Using Art Clay Silver 650 Overlay Paste

We've talked previously about what SOL Paste is and its general use. However, let's get into some specifics.

650 SOL Paste is formulated expressly for use on unglazed and glazed porcelain. Because porcelain is so dense and its high-fired glazes so unforgiving, 650 SOL Paste is just that much more successful on non-porcelain ceramics such as terra cotta. 650 SOL Paste can be used with a paintbrush, in an airpen, and in the previously mentioned sgraffito (stenciling) technique. Examples using 650 SOL Paste to its finest advantage include:

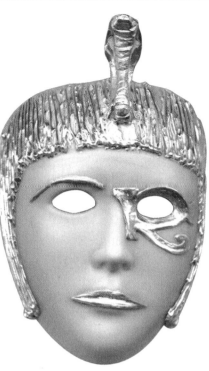

Art Clay Silver on bisqueware is more successful when used on larger areas.

- On porcelain bisque dolls as jewelry and accessories.

- On glazed porcelain cabochons and beads for jewelry.

- On glazed porcelain accessories such as picture frames, nametags, spoons, cups and saucers for personalized or unique designwork.

- As an extension, because you can fire 650 Overlay Paste at 1200° for 30 minutes, it's great for firing over glass as well.

The important things to remember are to clean your porcelain thoroughly prior to adding Art Clay 650 SOL Paste, and to fire your porcelain more slowly, at either 1000°F or 1500°F/hour. That also means you have to cool your pieces slowly as well. For all practical purposes, it's enough to keep the kiln door closed following completion of the cycle until near room temperature. Removing the porcelain prematurely will crack it due to thermal shock.

Stage Two—The Greenware State

Drying
Air drying—not too much to be said here. You form it, you walk away. How long? Well, that's the kicker. If you live in Miami, it might take two days. In Utah or Death Valley it might only take five minutes. Seriously, air drying means just that. The upside is that it's cheap; you don't need any further hardware. The downside is that it's unpredictable. And nearly any method you use to speed drying will save you time. Besides, I like to be in control; in classroom situations, control of time is essential.

**Remember, Art Clay Slow Dry takes five times longer to dry than regular clay.

NOTE:
To create a mirror finish it is most important that the initial filing get rid of the pitting and imperfections before using wet sandpaper. Patience in sanding with 600, 1200, and 2000 grit sandpaper, rinsing the sandpaper often, and sanding evenly will make the difference between a beautiful piece and an extraordinarily gorgeous piece.

Use a stainless steel net to keep your fingers cool while drying a project.

Hot air dryer, otherwise known as a hairdryer—there are many sizes, shapes and wattages. Most get the job done. Some disadvantages:

- You should get a stainless steel net to hold your pieces while you dry them. Holding the wet clay in your hand while you dry is dangerous and you'll quickly find any hairdryer is too hot for this method. I much prefer the Teflex sheet.

- You have to hold the dryer to dry. A quick tip is to get a small cardboard box, cut off all the flaps, and lay the box on its long side. Cut a hole slightly smaller than the diameter of your hair blower nozzle in the center of the top. You can then insert the nozzle of the hairdryer, place your pieces inside the box, and, setting the dryer on low or medium, enjoy hands free drying.

- Certain hair blowers are so hot that they quickly dry the outside of a thick piece, which will become hot to the touch, while the inside remains moist. If fired, the moisture will expand and rupture the surface of the piece.

Toaster Oven—the kind nearly everyone has had in closets, cupboards, cabinets and, probably, garage sales. Some advantages and disadvantages:

- You have to be careful not to let toaster ovens get too hot. 150°F to 175°F is the most you should allow. Anything above that and you risk the binders of the dried clay beginning to burn off.

- The interiors can be plenty roomy for multiple layers and pieces.

- They're generally portable; great for classes.

- They can draw a lot of power.

- There isn't any air flow of air; they're just mini-ovens.

Griddle, hot plate, or food warmer—again, food warmers are few and far between these days and generally have to be dug up from the depths of "abandoned kitchen appliance" limbo. For all, however, here are some pros and cons:

- All are temperature controllable—a good thing, but the same caveat as for other appliances.

- All are also flat. Terrific for flat Art Clay pieces, but a disadvantage when trying to dry dimensional objects.

Food Dehydrator—make no bones about it, this is the best choice for the money. I normally try to be non-partisan, but Patricia Walton, one of Art Clay's Directors of Education and I saw something like it when we were obtaining our Masters Training in Japan. It was a clear glass chamber, and instructors and R&D people at Aida Chemical Industries were constantly putting Art Clay Silver pieces in and taking them out. We asked what it was and we were told it was a drying chamber. Trish and I looked at each other and she said "food dehydrator!" On returning to the States, I did extensive online research, looking for the one food dehydrator that would meet the needs of Art Clay students and instructors. The result is the Excaliber® brand of food dehydrator. Here are some advantages of food dehydrators, in general, and the Excaliber in particular:

Excaliber's nine-tray food dehydrator is the perfect answer for teachers and students alike.

- It's light. Whether you get the four-, five-, or nine-tray model, it's extremely portable and uses regular household current. With the Excaliber, you get removable trays to accommodate ring mandrels or larger pieces. The shelves have plastic grids to allow air circulation.

- There is a temperature control, but the highest is around 150°F, a perfect temperature. No danger of overheating.

- There is air circulation. This is the single most important factor, and the reason the food dehydrator is superior to all other drying forms. Air circulates throughout the interior, removing moisture at the same time it's drying. After all, if you were using bananas and apricots instead of Art Clay, that's what you'd want, isn't it?

- With the Excaliber model, the fan is in the rear of the machine instead of the bottom. This allows for even drying. With other store models, the fan is on the bottom and the pieces on the bottom tray would dry sooner than those on the top. The Excaliber has a great fan in the back that sends hot air forward over all the pieces evenly. In my nine-tray model, it takes about 10 minutes to dry just about any size piece my students make.

TIP:

You can tell if a piece is dry by placing it onto a flat piece of metal or plastic. A halo of condensation will appear under the piece if it's not dry.

Pre-Finishing

Filing and sanding are what you've been waiting for. You've shaped your piece, dried it, and now it's time to get it just the way you want it. This is the stage where you can take all the time you want, or need. Did a piece develop a crack? You can fill it and dry it again. Forgot to add a finding or that do-dad you made? No problem. Add a little Art Clay Silver paste and attach it. Getting the piece all spiffy and ready for firing is my favorite time.

Files

No doubt there are hundreds of different files in shapes, cuts, and degrees of fineness. If you have large scratches or gouges, rough edges and "ugly places," a file is what you want to use first. Tips for using files:

- Use the right shape for the right job. If you're trying to smooth a rough hole, don't use a flat file. It's worth investing the $4+ in a mini-file set to get the shape you need and save the grief of a broken piece.

- Keep the file clean. Art Clay Silver dust is very fine. Every minute or so, take whatever file you're using and tap it to clean it, or take a stainless steel brush and gently brush the file teeth. You'll find it works faster and more efficiently. Also, a light application of olive oil will keep your files from rusting.

- Check your filing OFTEN. It's easier to check how much clay you've filed off than it is to try to replace a big gouge you've made because you got carried away.

- Rule of thumb: Use files just to remove large defects and to attain general shape. Files don't smooth, they remove.

Sandpaper

There are many different types, but we're only going to discuss one kind here, standard silicon. The basic Art Clay curriculum teaches the use of three sizes of grit: 600, 1200,

Use the right file for the right job.

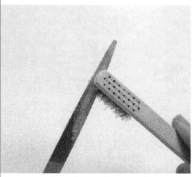
Remove fine dust with a stainless steel brush.

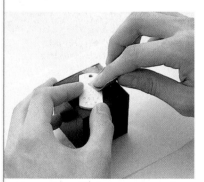
Use a rubber block as a support whenever possible. It will decrease chances of breaking your piece while filing and sanding.

and 2000. The first can be found at most hardware stores, the second, at select specialty hobby or hardware stores. The finest grit sandpapers are available only through craft and specialty jewelry stores. Grades such as fine, ultrafine, superfine, and microfine, are all subjective, so check carefully to make certain you have the finest grits you need to achieve the level of smoothness you're looking for. Generally, any number lower than 1200 grit (300, 400, 600, etc) removes silver. In jewelry parlance, this is considered grinding. With grits 1200 and higher (1500, 2000, 4000, etc.) you are not removing clay or silver, you're creating successively finer and finer scratches. Or, more accurately, you're polishing, not sanding. Here are some guidelines:

- If you are planning to create a mirror finish, use grits no higher than 1200 prior to firing. Of course, you could go higher, but there wouldn't be any point. You'd lose any finer sanding in the sintering process.

- Like the files, clean your sandpaper frequently, especially the finer grits. Do this by gently brushing the sandpaper onto a separate surface, such as Teflex or Acetate. These clay particles can then be recycled into your paste container.

- Keep a stiff-bristled brush, such as a short stenciling brush, handy to brush the excess silver dust onto your work surface. NEVER blow the dust from your piece. Not only does this send the dust particulates into the air where they might be inhaled, but it's a waste of good silver!

- To sand surfaces level, such as ring sides that must be kept even, place the sandpaper on a flat surface, such as a rubber block or your work surface, and rub your piece against the sandpaper rather than the other way around.

- Finally, try wiping your finished greenware piece with a slightly damp cosmetic sponge. This will smooth the surface and remove the last vestiges of silver dust, making your post-firing work much easier. The cosmetic sponge can be rinsed in a separate container and the silver reclaimed through evaporation.

Stage Three – Firing and Post Firing

Firing

Firing is how clay turns into pure silver. This is where it all happens. Everything else you've done has been a prelude to this bit of technological alchemy. No matter which method you use to fire Art Clay Silver, the process is the same: burning the organic binders off and sintering the silver particles to increase strength. In the end, you have a piece of 99.9 percent fine silver with the strength of 18k gold, just 8 percent to 10 percent smaller and with all the fine detail and shape of the prefired greenware.

Gas Stovetop—five minute firing. This is the easiest and least expensive method of firing Art Clay Silver (unless you don't have a gas stove, of course). All you need is a stainless steel net at least 4" square, a pair of tweezers, and a timer. Here's a summary of the firing procedure:

1. Place net on cold burners.

2. Turn on burner full flame.

3. Visually note where the cherry red, hottest parts of the net are.

4. Turn off the burner.

5. Using tweezers, place the dried, Art Clay Silver piece on one of the places that glowed the hottest.

6. Observe when the small amount of smoke and flame coming from the piece has ceased, and the piece has begun to glow. Set the timer for five minutes.

7. Following completion of the firing, turn off the gas to the stove and allow the piece to cool naturally for at least 20 minutes.

8. With tweezers, transfer piece to a metal basin of cold water and complete the cooling process.

9. Dry and finish as desired.

Note where areas of the net glow hottest and place your piece there.

Butane Torch—between 1 to 4.5 minutes firing time. There has been some debate about the necessity of using butane over other gasses, i.e. propane, acetylene, etc. Art Clay's official response:

Firing with a torch involves using visual cues to maintain the piece at the appropriate sintering temperature. Most important among these cues is the color of the metal. The sintering temperature range for Art Clay Regular and Slow Dry is 1472°F for 30 minutes or 1600°F for 10 minutes. The melting point for silver remains 1760°F. The torch Art Clay World, USA, sells has a flame rating from 1400°F to 2000°F. This butane torch was chosen for several reasons:

Firing Art Clay Silver with a butane torch is fast and easy.

• It is easily refillable using commercially available fuel, i.e. butane for cigarette lighters.

• The chosen torch contains safety features that allow easy, safe operation by qualified adults and supervised younger students.

• The flame, once initiated by the user, needs little-to-no adjustment in order to function adequately.

• The use of butane for firing has been carefully researched; the sintering process using butane is regulated by the torch used, and the results of firing with butane are consistent and reproducible.

That said, and remembering that the cue for torch firing is the color of the metal, there is no reason other gasses can't be used to fire Art Clay Silver with adequate and successful results. However, using propane and other fuels requires more than a passing knowledge of the equipment, gasses and how to use them safely to achieve the same results as using butane. For that reason, Art Clay World, USA can only recommend the use of the torch with which it is familiar and for which safety testing has been performed.

Here, then, is the equipment needed: refillable butane torch, a metal pan, a fiber/firing brick (compressed, refractory ceramic fiber), tweezers, timer or watch with second hand, and a metal or ceramic basin or cup with cool water.

1. Place the brick inside the metal pan.

2. Set the dried Art Clay piece on the brick. If your piece contains any small gemstones, make sure that they are faced away from the direct flame of the torch.

3. Fill and light the butane torch according to manufacturer's directions.

4. Hold the torch at a 45° angle at approximately. 1" to 2" distance from the piece.

5. Keep the flame on the piece at all times, rotating slowly to heat the piece evenly.

6. Observe as the small bit of smoke and flame signal the combustion of the organic binders. After this is completed, the piece will begin to turn white. Watch the piece carefully.

7. Observe in a dimmed light, or shaded area, as the piece begins to glow. The visual cues at this point are very important. The color must be a peachy orange, and not a deep, intense orange or cherry red. If the piece begins to shine, or the surface bubbles at all, increase the distance between the flame and the piece immediately, as this signals imminent melting.

8. When a peachy glow has been established, adjust the distance between the flame and the piece to maintain that color and start your timer or observe the second hand of your watch.

9. Remember that a piece from 1gm to 2gms requires a minute of firing time; from 2gms to 5gms, 1.5 minutes; from 5gms to 10gms, you need to fire for at least 2 minutes; from 10gms to 15gms, 2.5 minutes; from 15ms to 20gms., 3 minutes; and from 20gms to 25gms, 3.5 to 4 minutes. The official temperatures from Aida Chemical Industries have been less than that, but it is our experience at Art Clay World, USA, that the times given here are more realistic and will result in a more completely fired and stronger piece.

10. When the appropriate firing time has been completed, turn off the torch and place it in a safe location, as it is still very hot. Using a tweezers, grab the hot piece securely and set on the metal tray for a minute or so to begin the cooling process. You can leave the piece here to cool naturally or, if the piece is consistent in shape, you can pick it up and submerge it into the cool water. Depending on the residual heat within the piece, it may sputter or sizzle. Once that has stopped, the silver is cool enough to remove, dry, and begin the finishing process.

In summary, there are advantages and disadvantages in using either the stovetop or butane torch method:

- Both are relatively inexpensive to use.

- Both methods are easily portable.

- Only one piece can be fired at a time with each.

- Only silver and small stones can be fired with either. You cannot fire glass and/or ceramics with either the torch or stovetop method. The sudden, direct heat would cause thermal shock of the materials.

- Size limitations restrict clay to 25gms total weight and the size of a United States silver dollar—anything larger and heavier, and the complete sintering of the material would be doubtful. If organic materials are not completely burned out and the particles of silver cannot bond together, the finished piece will remain brittle and breakage could occur much more easily.

Kiln Firing

Kiln firing is the most accurate method of firing Art Clay Silver or Gold. It also requires either the rental of kiln time or the purchasing of a programmable kiln, i.e., one capable of being programmed for the specific temperature and time necessary to complete the sintering process. Since there are several kiln manufacturers and models capable of performing this procedure, we will only mention the kilns that Art Clay World, USA, distributes and recommends. Paragon kilns and, specifically, the SC-2 or SC-3 programmable kiln model. Paragon sells, and Art Clay also distributes the Caldera kiln, which differs from the SC series in that it is a top loader and has fiber brick sides and exposed elements inside. This makes the Caldera heavier, slower to heat and slower to cool. It's advantage is that it is rated for much higher firing, up to 2300°F. It also has an optional collar which, when placed below the main chamber, allows for bead annealing and increased chamber size.

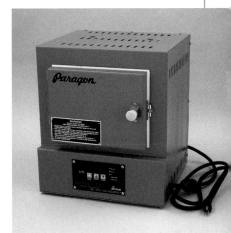

Paragon's SC-2 programmable kiln is the most recommended model for Art Clay Silver users.

Most firing situations, however, will be adequate using the more compact, lighter SC-2, front loading model. It, too, is computer programmable, and has the added advantage of having the five most common ramping speeds preprogrammed into its software.

There are specific firing temperatures and procedures for the various forms of Art Clay Silver. All can be broken down into two categories: those that can be fired from a hot kiln, and those that must be fired from a cold (or room temperature) kiln. Within those two categories there are obvious subcategories, which we'll go through.

Cold Kiln Firing

There are two types of Art Clay Silver that must be fired from a room temperature kiln. The main reason for this is that the amount of time it takes to go from a "cold" kiln to the required sintering temperature is actually a part of the sintering process. Therefore, if you should put either one of these types of Art Clay into an already warm kiln (above 300°F) and continue the cycle from there, the finished piece will not be as strong and may actually break or crack during normal wear and tear.

According to Aida Chemical Industries instructions, you need to put your greenware pieces into a room temperature kiln, ramp up normally to 1472°F, turn off the kiln and simply allow the kiln to cool naturally. When the internal temperature of the kiln reaches 300°F, you can remove the completed pieces. In the case of 650 Overlay paste, the ramping action and the temperature stall at 1472°F (after the kiln is turned off and before the heat begins to dissipate) are engineered into the sintering process. When firing to the alternate temperature of 1250°F, it is similarly important that the pieces be ramped from a room temperature kiln, and the kiln held at 1250°F for 30 minutes. To alter either, by removing the piece early or by shortening the "ramp-up" speed, will result in an under-fired piece.

The only other caveat here is a reminder that if you have a large piece of ceramic or porcelain over which you have used the SOL paste, you need to take that into consideration when deciding how fast to ramp the kiln to the proper sintering temperature. Remember that porcelain should not be heated quickly or it may crack. This, however, is a separate factor from the Art Clay Silver instructions but must be considered as an important component in the successful firing of the overall piece.

It is very important to fire Paper Type pieces of substantial size (not just small appliqué-sized bits) in a room temperature kiln, taking more than 15 minutes to bring it up to full firing temperature. It takes my SC-2 one half hour to reach 1600°F from room temperature, so this is normally not a problem. And, top firing temperature for Paper Type is 1472°F with a soak (hold) time of 30 minutes. Similarly, you should allow finished Paper Type pieces to cool naturally.

Normal Kiln Firing
Regular and Slow Dry Clays can be placed either into room temperature kilns or kilns already above 300°F. In fact, if you have classes, you can keep your kiln at 1600°F all day and, providing your greenware pieces are dry and contain nothing that would thermal shock, you can put on protective gloves, use a spatula or tongs, and load a piece of fiber board with your prepared pieces on it every 10 minutes. You can open the door, remove one load and immediately insert another. Of course, you must wait until the thermostat reads 1600°F again before timing for 10 minutes. Are there exceptions? You bet!

- Anything containing cork clay as a hollow form must be placed into a kiln with a temperature lower than 400°F. Why? Because the cork needs to be allowed time to burn off, and at temperatures higher than that, the cork will burst into flames even before you get a chance to close the kiln door and alter the firing parameters enough to endanger the successful firing of your piece.

- Oil Paste must also be allowed to take a certain amount of time to reach proper firing temperature. Remember that Oil Paste is never used on greenware, only on fired silver. Therefore, there are no water-based organic binders to burn off. In order for a proper repair or weld, adequate heating time must be allowed.

It's worth repeating that any Art Clay Silver that includes glass, ceramics, fireable gemstones or porcelain cannot be heated too quickly—or, for that matter, cooled too quickly.

Cooling—How Patient Do You Have to Be?
Art Clay Silver Regular, Slow Dry and 650 Low Fire can all be removed from the kiln

as soon as it is cool enough to do so.

When the kiln alarms, shut off the alarm and crack the kiln. The interior will be glowing red. Allow the glow to dissipate and use a welder's glove and a spatula or tongs to remove your pieces to a safe area, on a fiberboard, stainless steel net, or other protected area. If fired with a torch or on the gas stovetop, the instructions are similar.

If glass is present when using Art Clay Silver Regular or Slow Dry, crack the kiln and allow the temperature to drop to 1050°F or so. Close the kiln door immediately, and do not open it again until it is near room temperature. Why? "Crash cooling" will stop the glass from retaining heat and continuing to soften. At higher firing temperatures, some glasses de-vitrify, forming crystals that muddy or cloud the original glass' colors and this procedure prevents that.

Opening the kiln door between 1050°F and about 650°F may interfere with the glass' proper annealing (stress-releasing) procedure, especially if there is silver present. Should you open the door more than a second or so accidentally, the safest solution is to allow the piece to cool and then re-fire the entire piece to the original firing temperature, following correct cooling procedures. This will release any stress that was accidentally captured in the glass during the initial annealing cycle.

Ceramics and porcelain are handled similarly, without the annealing worries. The only concern is heating or cooling too quickly and thermal-shocking the ceramics. This is especially important if firing with Art Clay Silver. Remember that the silver has contracted 8 percent to 10 percent and as soon as the door is opened, the silver will loose heat quickly. The ceramics, on the other hand, lose heat more gradually … and the combination is an invitation for disaster. While a cracked piece of glass can always be re-fired at fusing temperatures until healed, ceramics aren't as forgiving, and a crack is a crack forever.

Finishing

The Art Clay Silver is fired, it's cool and dry. Now you're staring at this finished, one-of-a-kind artwork you've created and you're thinking, "What the heck is all this white coating, and where's the silver?"

The coating is not fire scale, it's not even oxidation; it's a layer of silver molecules which have been irregularly arranged. It's going to take—that's right—*finishing*, to bring the silver to the surface. If you've all done your jobs properly, finishing the piece should be a warm, Tucson breeze (as opposed to a frigid Chicago gale, but we won't go there).

There are many different ways to finish your fired Art Clay Silver piece, and we're going to touch on the most common. Unless we specify otherwise, assume all finishes are by hand.

Brushed Finishes
Brushed finishes create scratches on the surface of the piece. The direction and material used determines the kind of finish.

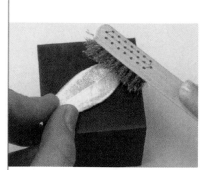

Use a stainless steel brush to make a matte finish.

Rotary tumblers require shot, water and some kind of jewelry cleaning compound.

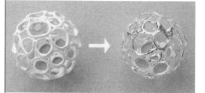

Tumbling for at least 1½ hours will turn white to wonderful.

Stainless steel is the most common. Brushes with these bristles are normally used to remove the white coating after firing. This leaves a matte finish that can be attractive all by itself.

The *brass* look is similar to stainless steel, but softer, almost satin.

The difference between *florentine* and other finishes is that the scratches are not random brushings, but purposefully placed parallel with cross-cut markings. The pattern is very fine, and very classy if done well.

The *tumbled finish* is one of the easiest. There are four basic kinds of tumblers.

1. The Rotary tumbler uses a rock tumbler but instead of rocks, you add some mixed shape, stainless steel shot (different shapes of small, stainless steel pieces), water, and non-ammoniated jewelry cleaner. Drop your fired Art Clay pieces in, close the chamber, and turn the machine on. The machine rotates slowly, the steel shot hits the piece repeatedly, work-hardening and burnishing the surface into a shine. Typically, a rotary tumbler takes 1.5 to 2 hours to shine silver.

2. With the Vibratory tumbler, the chamber vibrates back and forth. Instead of a mixed shape shot, the most common vibratory shot is called "pin" shot. There is usually a knob that controls the speed of the vibrations. Caveat: If the vibrations are too fast, the efficiency drops.

3. Magnetic tumblers utilize a rotating magnet in the base and steel needle shot to finish in a fraction of the time. However, if work-hardening your piece is an important part of the finishing process, this may not be the best method of choice.

4. Ultrasonic tumblers use ultrasonic vibrations to clean the silver. A HUGE caveat, here! There are many gemstones for which the ultrasonic tumbler spells certain doom, emeralds being one, opals another. In fact, any stone that has imperfections should stay away from ultrasonics.

Note: There is no doubt that tumbling silver creates a shiny surface. However, shiny does not make smooth. A true, professional shine takes more than a couple of hours in a tumbler. As any jeweler will tell you, it's hard work.

The *mirror* finish is the Rolls Royce of finishes. There is a certain level of skill in producing a true, hand made, "see yourself" mirror finish, and Art Clay World, USA teaches this technique in every certification class. The secret to a fine polish is patience. You will be putting successively finer and finer scratches in the surface of your piece. You'll need 600, 1200 and 2000 grit sandpaper, a rubber block, a small dish of clean water and some Wenol silver polish. You'll also need baking soda and a polishing cloth.

1. Prepare your piece by brushing with a stainless steel brush to create a matte finish.

2. Take a piece of the 600 grit sandpaper and wet it thoroughly. Place the piece on the rubber block and rub evenly in one direction. Use some muscle and pressure. Keep the piece wet and the sandpaper free of grit. Continue to rub until the entire area to be shined is covered in even scratches and there is no more resistance to the sandpaper.

3. Use clean water with each change of sandpaper. Rinse the piece well, and wet the 1200 grit sandpaper. Rub the piece in the opposite direction with the 1200 grit. Rinse the sandpaper and the piece often and continue until there is no more resistance.

4. Change water again. With the wet 2000 grit sandpaper, and a lot of elbow grease, rub in small circles until you begin to see a shine. As always, keep your sandpaper rinsed well.

5. After you've finished with the sandpaper, rinse one last time and dry thoroughly. Put a very small amount of Wenol silver polish on the polishing cloth and rub firmly and evenly. What you thought had been a shine will turn into the most beautiful mirror finish you've ever seen.

6. Make a paste of a small amount of baking soda and water and rub into the piece. This will remove all traces of the Wenol without removing the shine. Rinse one last time and buff with a clean, soft cloth. Wow!

Nothing can match the pride felt by creating a professional, mirror finish by hand.

Patinas
They're all about contrast. People use patinas on their finished jewelry pieces for a number of reasons:

- It covers up imperfections and makes things appear "rustic" or antiqued.

- It makes detail more apparent because the patina darkens the cracks and crevices.

- It increases contrast between textures and decorative elements.

There are several patina brands on the market that will work on pure silver.

Silver Black does just that: it makes the silver black. You submerge the finished silver piece into the Silver Black until the whole piece is covered, then remove, rinse and dry. To create highlights, you have to remove the patina agent on the surface using a brush or polish. This will restore the silver finish on surface areas and leave the black in recessed areas. The alternative method is to use a paintbrush and carefully paint the Silver Black into the desired areas.

Liver of Sulfur—the name says it all. The color of bile, a smell of rotten eggs so strong it will curl the hair off a mouse. LOS comes in a can of small chunks, or premixed into a liquid. Unfortunately, *nothing* works as well, or gives the range of colors on pure silver as does Liver of Sulfur. You just have to know how to use it.

Dry chunks are better to use than premixed liquid. LOS is light sensitive and has a definite shelf life once mixed. Also, you can control the dilution with the dried chunks. Here's Art Clay's procedure for using Liver of Sulfur on fired silver:

1. Any residual oils or contaminants will interfere with the LOS reacting with the silver. So, clean your piece thoroughly with a paste made of baking soda and water, and rinse.

TIPS:
For a perfect mirror finish: If you have scratches that you can't remove with 600 grit, going to a 1200 grit won't make them any better. You have to go *back* a step to remove imperfections. Use a file until the scratches are gone, *then* go forward again. You'll have a much easier time if you remember to sand with 600 and 1200 grit sandpaper *before* you fire.

Dip the cleaned piece into the Liver of Sulphur solution until the piece attains the desired color.

Remove and rinse well.

Remove the surface patina with Wenol on a soft cloth. Dark recesses will add definition.

2. Heat a pint (one cup) of clean water until it's steaming, not boiling. Have another cup of cool rinse water immediately handy, as well as a clean towel, some ammonia, and stainless steel tweezers or a scrap of wire. Do NOT use aluminum.

3. While the water is still steaming, take a thumbnail-sized chunk of liver of sulfur and drop into the hot water. Add several drops of ammonia. Stir with a plastic coffee stirrer until dissolved. The solution should be the color of coffee.

4. On pure silver, the patina colors on Liver of Sulfur are a result of heat and time. Therefore, the stronger, hotter solution will act very quickly. As the solution cools, the Liver of Sulfur becomes less potent and takes longer to react. The colors will appear in this order: gold, deep gold, magenta, niobium blue, and black.

5. Take hold of the piece of silver with a tweezers or, if there is a hole, thread the scrap wire through it. The goal is to make sure you have a firm hold on your piece.

6. Dip the entire piece into the hot solution and immediately remove it and dip it into the cool water to rinse and stop the reaction. Your piece should be at least golden, with other color highlights depending on how fast you were.

7. From this point on, you determine how much color you want on your piece. You can continue to dip the entire piece, or use a paintbrush to put the solution exactly where you want it.

8. If the solution begins to lose potency, reheat it in the microwave for a few seconds

9. Make sure you have plenty of ventilation. The intense odor of LOS (not to mention the ammonia) will linger a long time after it's gone.

10. Every time you rinse your piece, wipe it with the towel or you'll dilute your solution when you re-dip.

11. When you've finished using the LOS solution, you can dispose of it by pouring it down the sink followed by cold, running water. LOS is sulfurized potash, so it isn't an acid and won't hurt your pipes, only make them smell.

Using Power

Up until now, all of the techniques described have used traditional hand tools and methods. That is not to say that power tools for pre-finishing and post-finishing can't be used. But power tools may save time at the expense of a "hand feel." To be sure, this is a subjective statement and I, myself, have been known to use a flexible shaft on a mini-power tool. Nevertheless, I strongly suggest that you learn the hand techniques first; get the feel of the clay, what it takes to sand, carve, file, and polish by hand. Honestly, if I want a mirror finish, I still use wet sandpaper and a lot of rubbing. There's just something about a hand finish that can't be copied with a power tool. Not to mention the pride in having carried on metalworking traditions hundreds of years old. But, if you want power, there are certainly plenty of machines to choose from.

The mini-power tool. Examples are the Sears Craftsman® power tool, Dremel®, Fordham®, any number of others. If you have any of these and intend to use them for carving or polishing Art Clay Silver, either before or after firing, you'd do well to invest in a flexible shaft. This shaft is attached to the main motor body, and allows you to perform all the usual motorized tasks holding a light, pencil-thin extension. This is especially important if you are using techniques that require water, such as drilling holes in glass, or carving any manner of stones. The main motor is well away from the drill bits and therefore reduces the chance of electric shock.

Power tools can save time and energy when used properly.

There will always be the traditional *polishing belts* on lapidary and metalworking machines that metalsmiths have used since their inception. All of them use friction and various grinding grits, powders, and pastes to achieve the desired finishes. Tripoli, red rouge, and dozens of other products are used successfully on a daily basis. The decision to use any of these methods is purely a personal choice, and results from ability and availability on a number of levels.

Chapter Three

Gold, the Other Metal

Twenty-four karat gold foil over fired Art Clay Silver is a technique called Kuem Bu.

How to Slice the Price

As is stated in the glossary, a karat is $^1/_{24}$ of the whole of the gold, and marks the purity. Therefore, 22 karat gold is 22 parts gold, and 2 parts alloy. In Art Clay's 22k yellow gold, that alloy is silver. The alloy gives the gold strength and durability, but doesn't lessen the value of the clay. Sold in either 5gm or 10gm packets, the 22k gold clay carries a price dear enough to inspire ingenuity in prolonging its life. Consequently, working in solid clay is not as common as the alternatives.

Hollow forms involves creating a desired shape out of cork clay, and then covering it in a layer of gold clay or several layers of gold paste. The firing temperature is the same as when working in solid gold, 1814°F for one hour.

Vermeil is a terrific method of painting layers of Art Clay 22k Gold Clay in paste form over Art Clay Regular Clay greenware.

1. Take a pinch of 22k gold clay (it doesn't have to be soft), and add water drop by drop, using a spatula to mix thoroughly until a paste the consistency of cream is formed.

2. Use a paintbrush to paint a layer of the gold paste over the desired area of green-

ware. This can be anywhere from a small detail to the entire surface of a piece. Let dry completely.

3. Repeat two more times until three layers of gold paste have been painted on the greenware.

4. Torch-, stovetop-, or kiln-fire the piece as though you were only firing the silver. The thin gold layers will bond directly to the silver. Caution: if you paint the gold too thickly onto the greenware, the top layer may flake. If you wish to add more gold, wait until the piece is fired, paint another thin layer of paste, and refire, burnishing thoroughly when complete.

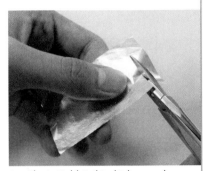

Art Clay Gold is most effectively used in small amounts.

Twenty-four karat gold foil is the perfect vehicle for hot embossing, known in metalworking as the Korean art of Kum Bu (or Keum Bu). Unlike many of the rather tissue-like 24k gold foils on the market, Art Clay's foil is thicker, and substantial enough to cut with scissors. The technique is easy and can be done with a kiln or hotplate. In either case, you need to start with a fired piece of silver that has been cleaned but not polished with Wenol or any other coating.

1. Cut the foil to the desired shape.

2. Dilute Elmer's or other non-toxic glue (no cyanoacrylate or "super" glues) and apply a very thin layer to the back of the foil piece.

3. Place the foil onto the silver and press gently. This is only to prevent the foil from "floating" away with the convection currents as the piece is heated.

4. Prepare a tong or spatula and a safe area to place the piece when it is removed from the heat. You will also need a protective glove, such as a suede welding glove, a long tweezer, and an agate burnisher. This is essential to permanently bond the gold onto the silver. An agate burnisher is polished agate attached with a strip of brass or other base metal to a bamboo handle. The agate is hard but gentle and does not conduct the heat away from the silver or gold.

5. If using a kiln, preheat the kiln to 1472°F. If using a hot plate, place the piece on the plate PRIOR to heating it. This is because the entire piece must heat up and be in direct contact with the plate while it is doing so.

6. When the kiln reads 1472°F, don the glove, open the door, and quickly place the silver piece with the foil attached into the kiln. Close the door quickly and watch the thermostat. When it again reads 1472°F, time for 2 minutes. At the end of 2 minutes, don your glove, open the door, and quickly remove the piece to the safe area. Immediately remove the glove and, holding the piece steady with the tweezer, use the agate burnisher to firmly burnish the gold to the hot silver piece. Begin in the middle and you will see the surface change as you burnish. Go out to the edges, careful not to trap air beneath the foil. Burnish all edges well. If the piece appears to cool and the edges are not yet adhering, return the piece to the kiln and repeat the above procedure. This can be repeated several times until all areas of the gold have been burnished and the gold is permanently embossed.

7. After you are satisfied with the result, allow the piece to cool naturally. Do NOT quench the hot silver and gold piece.

Art Clay's Gold Foil is thick enough to cut with scissors.

8. If using a hotplate, when the piece has heated to the proper temperature, you will notice a sudden change in the foil as it almost appears to be "pulled" against the hot silver. With your agate burnisher and a tweezers to prevent movement of the piece, you can carefully burnish the gold onto the silver while the piece is still on the hotplate. Again, once the piece is done, remove from the heat and allow to cool naturally.

9. Once your embossed pieces are cooled, you can complete the polishing process on the remaining silver. If done properly, this technique is permanent and striking. Adding the pure gold foil obviously also adds value to your piece.

Chapter Four

The *OOPS!* Factor, or the Art of Repair

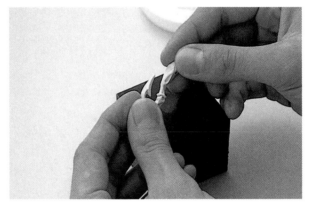

What *Can't* Be Fixed Prior to Firing?

In my experience, there is nothing—no crack, break, over-filing, under-filing, drilling or other "boo-boo"—that can't be fixed prior to firing, or *after* firing for that matter. But we'll take things one at a time.

In the greenware state, *cracks* are a snap to repair. I prefer to use the Syringe Type to fix cracks, as it has less water, is thicker, and dries more quickly. Remember to overfill the crack, allow the repair to dry, then file even with the rest of the piece.

Breaks are just as easy to repair. Put a layer of either Paste or Syringe type on both edges of the break and press firmly together. After holding for a minute, use a damp paintbrush to smooth the paste and dry thoroughly.

Forgotten findings—the findings most often forgotten to place are the flat screw-eye and the relatively new brooch pin screws. Usually, people forget to insert them into the wet clay. By the time they remember, the piece is dried greenware and they're cursing under their breath. Well, curse no more.

The flat screw-eye channel method—use a file to create a narrow channel perpendicular to the edge of the piece where the flat end of the screw-eye was supposed to go. Then squeeze a small amount of syringe into the channel and lay the screw-eye in place, press-

If done properly, no one will know you forgot to add the finding until after drying.

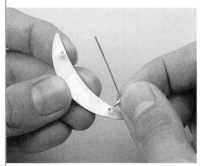

Setting the new model of brooch can be tricky if not planned properly.

ing gently. Smooth with a damp paintbrush and dry. Any noticeable bump can be sanded away.

Brooch Pin Screw Type findings—forgetting to press the two pure silver screw-fittings into the clay is not unusual, especially since it's a new technique and much different from that of the old, tab-style brooch findings. You have two choices:

- With a power tool or pin vise, and with a small grinding bit, carefully drill two holes where you want the fittings to go. Use Syringe Type to set them in place. Make sure that you attach the findings securely, but do not put paste onto the non-silver parts that unscrew prior to firing. Dry.

- Use a syringe to place a coil in the two spots where you want the two pure silver fittings. This coil technique very much resembles that used to set gemstones onto pre-fired clay. The coil must be high enough so that the screw type fitting is seated securely into the syringe clay, and the syringe clay is attached very securely to the greenware. **Caution**: if you do not bury the findings into the coils and paste them in well enough, they will come out after firing when you attempt to screw in the actual brooch findings.

After Firing—It's Not Over 'Til It's Over

Things happen. To everyone. The piece was too thin in spots, you pushed the bezel too far into the clay and the bottom cracked, you forgot to put a vent hole in that seahorse you pasted and now it looks like an alien baby has ripped its way out of the poor thing's chest cavity. But "Don't Worry. Be Happy." Every time you have to repair something, you learn a valuable lesson. And repairs are so easy (if frustrating) that you'll find yourself bemoaning the time you've lost rather than the actual difficulty of the repair. These aren't the only situations when you'll find repairs are needed, but they're probably the most common.

Art Clay has several products that will resolve *cracks in silver*. At the time of this writing, Oil Paste is the one product formulated exclusively for use on fired silver pieces. Think of it as spackle, or silver flux, or silver solder. In using it to fill cracks, you need to mix the paste very well and use a bamboo skewer or similar item to scoop up a portion. What is important for successful repair is to *roll* the Oil Paste into the crack so that no air is trapped. Tap the piece to force the Oil Paste into the crack, and overfill the crack. Remember that the surrounding silver is not going to shrink any more. It's already been sintered. The Oil Paste, on the other hand, still has to dry and contract 8 percent to 10 percent during firing. If you don't overfill, you'll find the crack will still be visible after re-firing. And remember, Oil Paste will take substantially longer to dry, and needs to be fired at 1472°F for 30 minutes.

Silver Overlay Paste is a relatively new product that allows the creation of beautiful silver designs directly on glazed porcelain. Because of the formulation, the paste is stickier than Art Clay Silver Regular paste, and can be used to repair pits and cracks similarly to using Oil Paste. One benefit of using SOL Paste is that it is water based, not oil based. It is 99.9 percent fine silver after firing, and has the same 8 percent to 9 percent shrinkage rate. SOL Paste fires to 1472°F from a room temperature kiln with no hold, or 1200°F with a 30 minute hold.

Those *breaks* not caused by trauma (stepping on your ring accidentally) are often caused by under-firing. Most often, this is following torch firing or stovetop firing. Why? Because kiln firing is, hands down, the most accurate method of firing. The other methods, torch and stovetop firing, depend on cues other than pyrometers and thermostats to tell us we've reached the appropriate temperature for the appropriate length of time. And, because those cues are visual and subject to all kinds of outside influences, the results might be less than optimal. To minimize the risk of post-firing breakage:

- When molding and/or shaping your piece in the wet stage, avoid trapped air and hidden creases in the clay that might weaken the piece after firing. The best way to do this is to knead the clay thoroughly into a tight ball prior to shaping your piece.

- When filing and sanding, avoid thinning your piece too much. Anything less than 1mm thick is considered insufficient and will be unstable after firing. Never forget that every Art Clay Silver piece will shrink 8 percent to 10 percent. Thin will become thinner, small will become smaller.

- Don't under-fire pieces when using the torch or stovetop. As long as you retain the correct color of the metal (peachy rose, not cherry red) you can extend the firing time for one minute or more. The single most important cue to the success of flame firing (torch or stovetop) is the internal color of the metal after the binders have burned off and the piece has turned white. If you start timing before the piece reaches that crucial stage, before the entire piece has become peachy pink, you will end the firing too soon. The silver will still contain minute pockets left by the burned out organic binders that will weaken it and increase the risk of breakage.

- Trace the outside of the piece on paper before firing. Compare the fired piece to the tracing, and if the finished piece is close to 10 percent smaller, you've fired correctly. If you do not see any change in size, simply refire the piece.

Repairing *cracks in fired glass* is a tough one. Once glass has cracked, whether it's due to incompatibility or thermal shock, there are only two ways to fix it.

1. Take the entire piece up to full fuse (1550°F to about 1625°F) and allow the glass to heal itself. If you have dichroic glass in your piece, it will probably shift colors again.

2. Crash cool the kiln to 1100°F and allow to cool to room temperature. Replace the glass. The easiest way to do this is heat your piece to about 1000°F, remove the piece, and quickly quench. The glass will shock and separate quickly from the metal. You can then cut another piece, insert it into the opening, and fire the piece again to above 1250°F (called tack fusing). Cool as described above.

Chapter Five

The Projects

MATERIALS

- 7 grams Art Clay, Original or Slow Dry
- Art Clay Paper Type (2.5gms – ¹⁄₄ sheet)
- Art Clay Paste Type (small amount)
- 4" x 4" sheet of Teflon for work surface
- Burnisher
- Cardboard or Plastic Slats at least 1mm thick, 2
- Roller
- Small plastic straw about 4mm - 5mm
- Flat paint brush
- Round paint brush
- Small cup for water
- Small container for thinned Paste
- Short bristle stainless steel wire brush
- 1" x 2" piece of 600 grit wet/dry sandpaper
- 1" x 2" piece of 1200 grit wet/dry sandpaper
- Soft polishing cloth
- Small amount of Wenol metal polish
- Small container with olive oil
- Plastic wrap, plastic bag, or Clay Keeper
- A selection of paper punches, scissors, craft knives, tissue or wave blades

Just the Clay, Ma'am

Basic Project

Rollover Bail & Applique Pendant

Patricia Walton

Seven grams of Art Clay is sufficient to create a pendant with a rollover bail about the size of a quarter. It is wise to decide on the shape of pendant and to have everything you need set up before you open the package of Art Clay. Art Clay begins to dry as soon as it is exposed to air. Art Clay Slow Dry will take five times longer to dry than Art Clay Original. In addition, it requires warming and conditioning with your hands for a few seconds before using. Successful rolling, forming and shaping are best accomplished when the clay is moist and pliable. Cracks and breakage occur when the clay begins to dry. Work quickly to achieve the basic shape and design. Once dry, you can take all the time you wish to file, sand and refine your creation.

To prepare your work area you will need the following; a small cup or bowl with water, 1" is sufficient. Have all the tools and supplies listed and your Art Clay and Art Clay Paste at hand. You will also want some plastic wrap, small plastic bag or Clay Keeper to store any left over clay. Place the Teflon sheet or other nonstick work surface in front of you. Position the two cardboard or plastic slats on top of and at the left and right sides of the Teflon sheet. This will allow you to roll out a uniform thickness. 1mm is the minimum thickness recommended for strength. Also before you begin, condition your hands using a very small amount of olive oil to help prevent the clay from sticking to your hands. You only need a light film on your hands. Condition your roller and straw by rubbing them in your hands. Too much oil will create a barrier between the clay sections and/or attached parts causing weak connections.

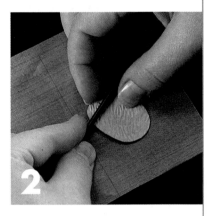

Instructions

1. Remove the Art Clay from the packaging; remember if you are using Slow Dry you must warm and condition it before proceeding. Form the clay into a ball and place in the center of the Teflon sheet. Quickly roll out the clay using the conditioned roller. The ends of the roller should rest on the slats to create a uniform thickness.

2. Lay the small straw onto the upper third of the rolled shape. Using your fingers or a damp flat brush pull the upper edge of the clay towards you, completely covering the straw until the edge is touching the clay surface. Press lightly. Seal and fill this area with a thick layer of Art Clay Paste applied with a round paintbrush. Smooth with a damp flat paintbrush. Check for cracks and fill with Paste if needed.

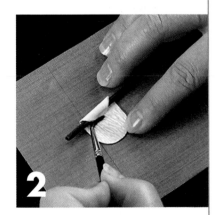

3. Completely dry the piece. Original Art Clay will only take a few minutes to dry if you use a dehydrator, hairdryer or warming tray. Slow Dry will take five times longer to dry. Air drying may take overnight to completely dry either Original or Slow Dry depending on your climate as well as the size and thickness of the piece. The ideal drying temperature is between 100°F and 200°F. Avoid higher temperatures as the binder may begin to break down, causing the piece to break before firing.

4. While the piece is drying you may cut out the appliqué design shapes from the Art Clay Paper Type using paper punches, scissors, craft knife, tissue or wave blade. (Tip: When using paper punches, turn the paper punch upside down so you can easily guide the Paper Type as well as see it as you punch.) The binder in the Paper Clay will degrade with moisture so take measures to keep it dry until you are ready to apply it to your piece.

Note: Art Clay Paper Type can also be scored and folded to create three-dimensional shapes such as created with Origami paper. An instruction sheet included with Art Clay Paper Type outlines how to use and fire when creating folding designs.

5. When the piece is completely dry, carefully remove the straw and check the roll over bail area. Add Paste to the inside of the bail area and check for and fill any cracks. Dry again.

6. You may choose either side as the front of the pendant or you can make it reversible with designs on both sides. File edges using a small fine file. Sand the edges using 600 grit sandpaper and smooth the entire piece using a damp makeup sponge. A damp sponge eye makeup applicator will smooth the bail area. The makeup sponge can be easily rinsed out in a small container of water and the Art Clay reclaimed. Until fired, all dust and leftover pieces of Art Clay can be reused.
   Note: The beauty of Art Clay is that you can do most of the finishing while the piece is in the "greenware" stage. Once fired the piece will need to be finished as you would any nonferrous metal which is harder to do and more labor intensive.

7. Place a tiny amount of the Art Clay Paste into a small container, adding an equal amount of water. Mix thoroughly with a brush. Apply a small layer of thinned Paste to the piece where you want the cutout and with your fingers, tweezers or a damp brush position the Art Clay Paper cutouts onto the piece. Gently press the cutouts onto the piece using your fingers. You want only enough Paste to adhere the cutouts. If the Paste is too thick the cutout will stick up and probably come off after firing. If any Paste gets onto the surface of the cutouts remove it by using a damp makeup sponge. If you do not remove it the cutouts will not be smooth and mirror finished after firing.

8. Allow the piece to air dry a few minutes while you prepare to fire using a torch or kiln. All pieces must be completely dry before firing. Any moisture in the clay will produce steam causing a small but dangerous explosion of hot particles. Do not use excessive heat to dry Paper Type.

9. Firing options:

   A. Torch firing. We recommend using a small butane kitchen torch. Be sure to read the instructions included with the torch to become familiar and comfortable with filling and using the torch. It is also recommended that you wear safety glasses anytime you are using a torch. Choose a well-ventilated area free of any combustible materials. A 12" x 12" or 18" x 18" square ceramic floor tile is a good heatproof surface on which to to place a metal pan containing a firing brick. You will also need a timer or watch as well as a pair of tweezers or tongs and a glass or metal container of water for final cooling of the piece. Place the dry Art Clay piece in the center of the firing brick. Light the torch and direct the flame approximately 1" to 2" from the piece. Keep the flame moving in a circular pattern around the piece. The distance and speed of movement will determine how fast the sintering temperature will be reached. The first thing you will observe will be some smoke and flame as the binder burns away. Continue to circle until the piece begins to glow orange. Dimming the lights makes it easier to see the color. This is the same glow necessary for annealing nonferrous metals. As soon as the glow appears, move the torch to a distance of 3" to 4", and begin timing for 1 ½ to 2 minutes. Larger pieces up to

Whether using a kiln or torch, all fired Art Clay Silver will appear white. When fired, Art Clay goes through a process called sintering; the resulting topography of the surface is one in which the micro particles of silver are randomly positioned (producing the white appearance) but when compacted via wire brushing, tumbling, burnishing or polishing the beauty of 99.9 pure silver is revealed.

the size of a half dollar will require up to 3 to 4 minutes to sinter. When the proper time has been reached, turn off the torch. The torch head is very hot so be careful where you set it. Also remember the firing brick and piece are very hot. You may remove the fired piece using tweezers or tongs to a metal surface or the floor tile to speed cooling time. Allow 10 minutes before dipping the piece in water. If you leave the piece on the firing brick to cool, allow 20 minutes before dipping the piece into the container of water. We do not recommend dipping the piece into water immediately after fusing as there is a risk of weakening, cracking or breaking.

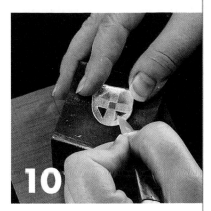

B. Paragon SC-2 kiln firing. Set the controller to Ramp 5, 1600°F, hold at 1600° for 10 minutes. Place the piece on a firing shelf, close the door and press to start. When the alarm sounds, turn off the kiln and open the door to cool. It will only take a few minutes to cool the piece.

10. You are now ready to finish and polish the piece. The piece will appear white. Brush the piece using a short bristle wire brush. Sand the edges using wet 600 grit followed by wet 1200 grit sandpaper. Create a mirror finish on the edges and cutouts using a burnisher. To polish and protect your piece use a small amount of Wenol metal polish on a soft cloth. Remove any residue with a clean soft cloth. The piece may also be finished using traditional metalsmithing techniques or a tumbler filled with stainless steel shot, water and jewelry cleaning solution. Finally, place your one-of-a kind creation onto a cord, chain or combine with your favorite beads.

Definition of sintering: "Sintering is the process through which ultra fine micro particles fuse or join together to form a monolithic, dense body, in the absence of large scale melting. Sintering frequently occurs at high temperatures, when atomic motion in the solid state is significant; sintering may occur in the presence of, or in the absence of pressure...The technology of producing ultra fine micro particles of pure silver and gold greatly reduces the sintering temperature to below the metals' melting temperatures. Therefore, the finer the particle, the lower the sintering temperature. Finer particles also result in a stronger particle bond when sintering."

Bringing Forth the GreenMan

Judi Hendricks

MATERIALS

- 2 to 5 leaves
- 20 to 30 grams of Art Clay Silver
- Teflex sheets
- Rolling guides
- Teflon roller
- Olive oil
- Craft knife
- Plastic wrap
- Water
- Paper towels
- Press mold for face
- Cotton swabs
- Art Clay Silver Paste
- Dehydrator
- Wet/dry sandpaper, 400, 600, 1200, 2000 grits
- Pre-moistened towelettes
- Fine silver bailback
- Art Clay Syringe type clay
- 20–20 gauge silver wire, ¹/₂"
- Tongs
- ¹/₂" wire brush
- Wenol silver polish

If you were to ask what influences my art, I'd have to admit that I'm a bit…well…squirrelly, in that I love trees and leaves. Especially leaves. (It's much harder to carry a tree home stuck like a flag in your hat.) Leaves fascinate me–they're a botanical marvel, of course, but even aside from that, I love the glorious shapes, the textures, and the colors for their pure aesthetics. Little leaves and big ones; delicate, fragile, translucent wisps of green and hearty plates of scarlet that whip down on a wet October day to slap you in the face and demand to be taken home. I love 'em! Every year as the seasons change, I begin to gather leaves. I've done this my entire life, much to the annoyance of my family. (I'm told that as a two-year old, my mother once lifted my pillow while making the bed and uncovered a veritable nest of leaves and twigs I'd hidden there.) In the autumn, bowls in my front hall brim with colored leaves, acorns, and pinecones. You can't pick up a book in my household without a pressed leaf fluttering to the floor, or an acorn that's been disturbed from some precarious balance skittering away across the tiles.

Add this to the fact that ever since I was a child I could "see" nature spirits (so did my grandfather—but he warned me that not everyone was lucky enough to have the ability), and you have an artist looking for a medium. The first time I used Art Clay Silver to make a "paste" image of a leaf and brushed clean the fired piece, I thought I could detect the faintest of pixie giggles ... which grew louder and stronger the more I explored the medium. My first GreenMan, *Mulberry Man*, was conceived during a walk I took with my dog. As I scuffed down the trail, a wet mulberry leaf clung to my sneaker-top. I reached down to dislodge it and I swear I could see a sprite's face in the leaf, winking

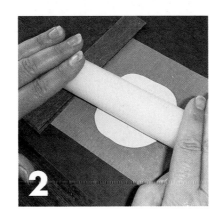

at me. I was so delighted by the whimsical image in my mind's eye that I didn't sleep until he was finished and hanging around my neck. (And, of course, from then on almost every leaf I met clamored for fine silver immortality!)

I can't teach you the magic of making Greenmen and Earthmothers, but I can describe the process. And if it draws you out into nature and has you peering beneath leaves and stems to find your spritely muse, then perhaps, if you're very quiet and listen carefully, these ancient earth spirits may come forward to tell you about themselves.

Instructions

1. Each of my pieces is made from real leaves, usually given to me by the trees themselves. I can't tell you how many leaves around Prairie Crossing—the conservation community in which I live—have literally stuck themselves to me as I walked the trails. Coincidence? Maybe; I prefer to think of it as earth magic.

   Depending on your design, you'll need two to five leaves; the design I'm showing here uses two mulberry leaves, each about 2¼" long. For practicality and weight, find leaves no longer than 2", or wider than 1". I prefer leaves that have a leathery texture to fleshier leaves, and—most importantly—the leaves you choose must have prominent veining on the underside. Mulberry leaves are wonderful for this, as well as for their curious and unique lobes. Make sure the leaves are clean and dry.

2. Prepare your rolling surface. I use Teflex sheets (used for cooking and candy making), but other non-stick rolling surfaces can work well too. I usually use a drop—and only a drop!—of olive oil rubbed lightly over the surface prior to rolling my clay.

   Most of my designs have used 20 to 30 grams of Art Clay Silver. (Mind you, I didn't plan to design them at that weight, but retrospective investigation has shown that I tend to design within that range. It makes for a nicely sized, solid piece with a substantial feel.) I use rolling guides and a Teflon roller to roll out my clay to an even 1.2mm sheet. This will give you leaves with enough mass to be shaped around your leaf-sprite face.

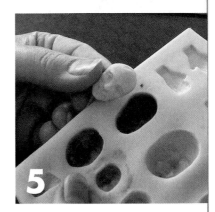

3. Working quickly, place the leaves face up on the rolled clay. (You want the ribbed underside in direct contact with the surface of the clay.) Remove the rolling guides and lightly roll the leaves into the clay until they are well embedded. And leave

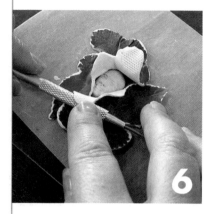

them there! Do NOT try to remove the leaves from the clay at this point.

4. Using a pin tool or a craft knife, cut away the excess clay and store it for later use. (My personal technique for storing Art Clay is to wrap it in plastic, wrap a moist paper towel around the plastic-wrapped clay, and insert the whole thing into a re-sealable plastic bag. I've kept stored clay moist for weeks this way.)

Cover your leaf/clay pieces with a moist paper towel and set them aside. Make sure they're well covered.

5. This could actually be Step 1, since it can be done ahead of time so that the face is dry and ready to place when your leaves are still moist but, in terms of placing the face, it falls in at Step 5.

The easiest way to make your GreenMan face is to use a lightly oiled press mold (of the kind intended for polymer clay use) available from any craft store. Again, I use a scant drop of olive oil on a cotton swab to prepare the mold prior to pressing the clay firmly in place. (And again, the amount of clay you'll use depends on the size of your leaf fairy's face.) If you're into mini-sculpture, you can sculpt a poly-mer clay face of your own, bake/cure it, and make a silicone mold from a two-part molding material, such as the kind Art Clay sells. I've even made a press mold from the face in an antique Cameo pin that took my fancy. You can also sculpt directly into the moist Art Clay, or carve/sculpt an image from a dried block of Art Clay. There are endless possibilities, so use your imagination!

I generally let faces dry in the mold (usually in a dryer/dehydrator) before unmold-ing them. Make sure there are no thin spots in the face. Check for blemishes or scratches in the surface of the dried clay and correct them now, before the face is placed in the piece. (Remember that with Art Clay, what you see is what you get! If there is an undesirable lump in the clay, there will be an undesirable lump in the fired piece. Clean it up now, while it's green clay and easy to manipulate.) If you want to tweak or fine-tune your sprite's facial expression, now is the time to do it.

6. I'm afraid this is where you step from craft into artistry … or fairyland. I "see" the faces of leaf-sprites in the leaves when I pick them up, so I know where the face is supposed to go. But if you're not lucky enough to spontaneously see fairy-faces, think in terms of balance, keeping in mind how the piece you're making is to be worn, and where you'll be placing the findings.

Place the leaf-covered clay sections in pleasing symmetry around the face, leaf-side up, pressing firmly. Once the individual sections begin to air-dry, you can lift them and "glue" them in place with Art Clay Silver paste-type clay or syringe clay. This demonstration piece is going to be a pendant hung from a bail-back at the top, so I'm placing the face slightly above center, curling the leaf-edges back to frame the face, like the cowl of a hood. You'll notice that I've also lifted the bottom leaf over a toothpick to provide textural interest, and curled the lower edge of the leaf slightly around my pin-tool to mimic the curl of a natural leaf. If you wish, the clay surfaces revealed by the curled-back leaf edges can be textured with a brush or pin tool.

Place the piece in a dryer/dehydrator at this point, and let it dry thoroughly (30 min-utes or more on high). If you haven't got a dryer/dehydrator handy, you can use a

  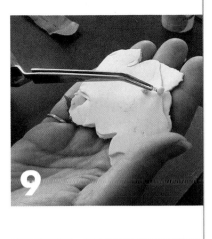

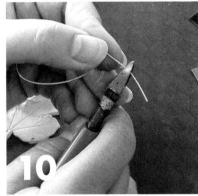

hairdryer, or let the piece air-dry in a warm (not over 200°F) place overnight.

7. When I took this demonstration piece from the dehydrator, the bottom leaf promptly disintegrated, leaving a lovely tracery of veins in its wake on the dried surface of the green clay. This is fine at this point (the leaf will often come off between drying steps and prior to firing), but try not to handle the surface of the leaf too roughly—you want to retain as much of that vein pattern as possible. At this stage, I will "decorate" my GreenMan with acorns, nuts, or berries made from Art Clay; this fellow gets a dragonfly companion glued beneath his chin with Art Clay Silver paste-type clay or syringe.

I'll then turn the piece over and add Art Clay Silver paste-type clay or syringe clay to the back to fill in gaps and strengthen the piece. I might have to do this three or four times, letting the piece dry thoroughly between each coat and checking to make sure that there are no unintentional holes or weak spots, particularly at the point where my bailback will be attached. (You want to have enough material laid down so that when you move to the next step—sanding and finishing—you can be confident of having enough material to sand to a smooth finish without sanding through the piece!)

8. When the piece is dry you can begin finishing the back with dry, 400 to 600 grit sandpaper to smooth out imperfections in the surface. The usual safety precautions apply to this stage: Do not inhale any of the silver clay dust (particle/vapor masks are always a good idea) and use a delicate touch when brushing dust from the surface of the piece (no blowing). Don't forget to retain all of your silver "dust" and reconstitute it in your paste jar, but make sure that you don't inadvertently pick up leaf particles that will contaminate your paste.

I'll warn you that it takes a little longer than the usual project to clean up the back of the GreenMan, because the face side of the piece is fragile in its green form and it's difficult to use a sanding block. But it's worth it, so persevere! Keep sanding, and move up in stages through 1200 grit sandpaper. When the back is smooth, give the piece a final "polish" by wiping down the back with a pre-moistened towelette.

At this stage, I'll take my pin-tool and etch my signature and a quality mark into the back of the piece. (Hint: it's much easier to do this right after you've wiped down the back with a pre-moistened towelette!)

9. Find the center of balance on your GreenMan piece and position the fine-silver bail-back finding at that point. (I use a dot or two of paste or syringe clay on the

face of the tabbed ends of the bailback to hold it in place.) Then apply a thick coat of Art Clay Silver paste-type clay or syringe clay to completely cover the tabbed ends of the bailback. Dry the piece thoroughly and check again. If you can see the tabbed ends, add more clay. Dry thoroughly and smooth lightly with a pre-moistened towelette.

10. I've seldom had good luck including the actual leaf stem with these pieces. They almost always fall off during the finishing stage. So rather than fuss trying to re-attach them, I make a new one.

I cut off a short length of fine silver wire (20 or 22 gauge) and, using my syringe's ribbon-tip, anchor it to the stem end of the leaf. This creates a secure (albeit tiny) armature over which you can pipe a new stem with your syringe.

Another trip to the dryer and—Ta Dah! A greenware GreenMan!

11. I usually kiln fire my GreenGuys, because many of them have rippling and curling leaves that need to be supported with firing batting as they sinter down. (I'm sure that, with care, they could be torch fired as well. Just make sure they're well supported!) There's no such thing as too much support—but remember that if you fail to give adequate support to any lifted detail it might well flatten out as it fires.

No special treatment here—just follow the Art Clay Silver label directions to fire out the piece.

So—the firing is done and the kiln has cooled to around 500°F. I love this part: To take base clay, pass it through the fire, and have it emerge from the flames as fine silver! This is magic! This is alchemy! You carefully maneuver your tongs to remove the piece from the kiln, toss it in the waters of the quench bucket, and hear the squelching hiss of hot metal and the Clunk! as the piece hits bottom. To me, this sound is the GreenMan equivalent of a baby's birth cry.

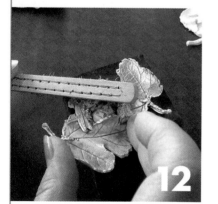

12. So there he is—all white and powdery-looking. I use both a ¼" and a ½" wire brush to remove the coating from the surface; the ½" brush is good to work beneath the cowl across the face. At this point I'll usually fine-sand the back of the

piece with 1200 to 2000 grit *wet* sandpaper or emery cloth to bring it to a high shine. If you want to work every trace of white free and bring it to a really high shine, you can also pop the piece into a tumbler with stainless-steel shot and a bit of burnishing solution for an hour or so. (Don't let it tumble too long or you'll soften the facial detail.)

13. Once my little man has been brushed free of residue (or tumbled), he goes back into the dehydrator. This is not only to make sure he's dry before applying the patina, but also to heat the piece. When applying Liver of Sulfur or a pre-mixed patina such as Silver Black, either the piece, or the solution, or both, should be hot. Since the finish I'm looking for is a simpler finish—I'm not going for iridescent peacock colors, but more of a pewter effect—I find it easiest (and most economical) to heat the piece and apply the Silver Black with a cotton swab. It's purely a matter of personal taste, but I patina only the front. I like being able to turn the piece over and show off the silver back.

14. When the piece is nicely darkened, I rinse it off in clean water to stop the chemical process. I then go back to my ½" wire brush to remove most of the patina, working in particular to highlight the face. Then a quick buffing with Wenol silver polish, and *voila*! Another GreenMan has been born.

To me, the echo of the majestic tree shows through in each of these miniature, wearable sculptures. These whimsical tree and leaf sprites, their origins rooted in ancient Earth lore, were magically crafted with real leaves—an ode to summer, which will never fade. Leaves … I just love 'em.

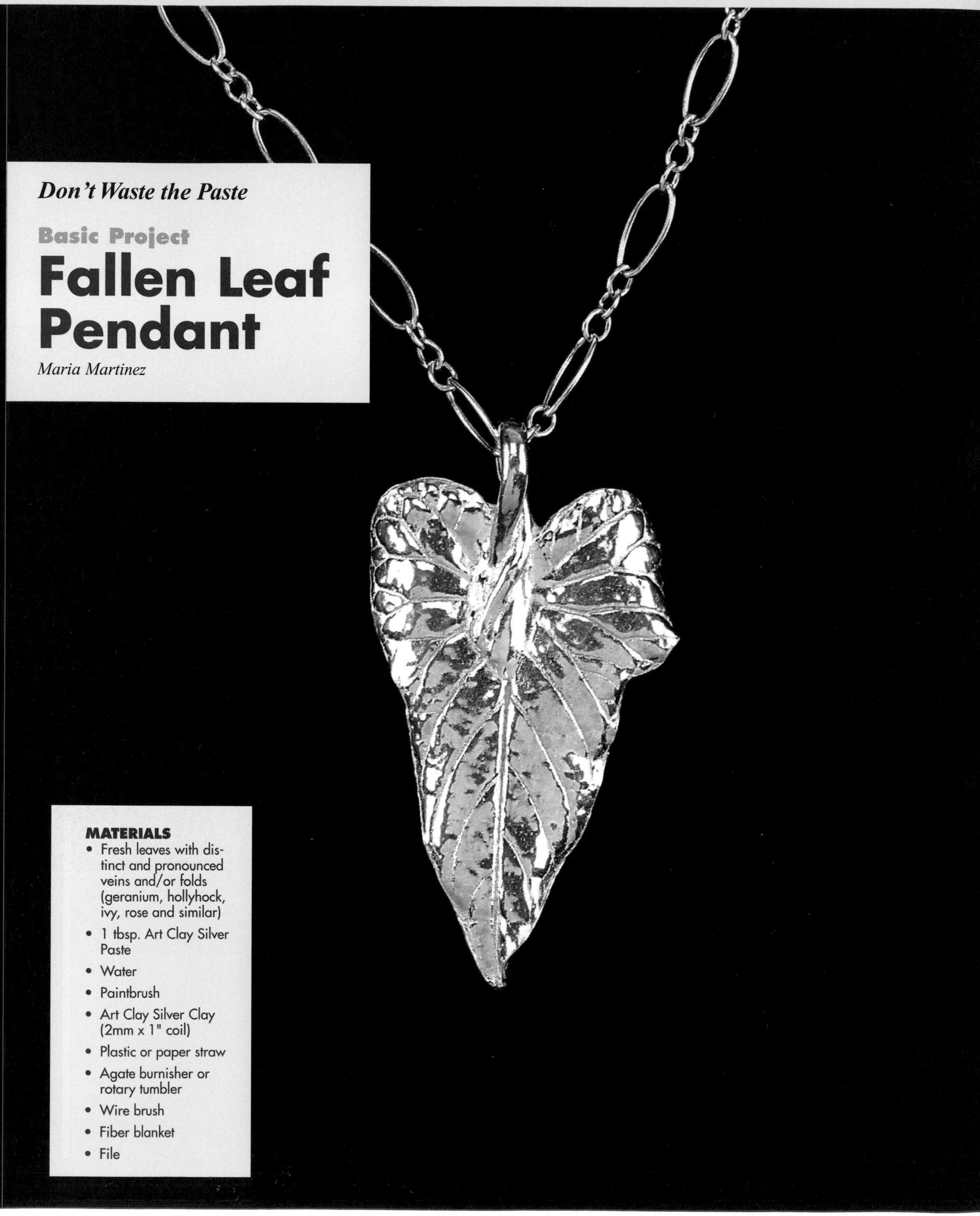

Don't Waste the Paste

Basic Project

Fallen Leaf Pendant

Maria Martinez

MATERIALS

- Fresh leaves with distinct and pronounced veins and/or folds (geranium, hollyhock, ivy, rose and similar)
- 1 tbsp. Art Clay Silver Paste
- Water
- Paintbrush
- Art Clay Silver Clay (2mm x 1" coil)
- Plastic or paper straw
- Agate burnisher or rotary tumbler
- Wire brush
- Fiber blanket
- File

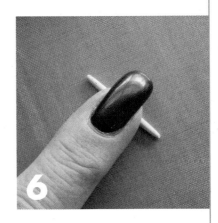

Instructions

1. Fresh leaves work best for this project. Keep them in a plastic bag with a few drops of water. Look for leaves with defined veins. Leave stems attached, as this will allow you to hold onto the leaves during the project. Do not use waxy or hairy leaves.

2. Take approximately 1 tbsp. Paste Type and place into a small container. Add water, drop by drop, until the consistency of thick cream. Stir slowly but do not whip as this will cause air bubbles. For the first few coats, the paste must be thin so it will settle into all the nooks and crannies of the leaf and create texture.

3. Apply the paste with a brush to the **underside** of the leaf. Make sure no leaf shows and there are no trapped air bubbles. Let dry. When applying additional coats, do not use a brushing motion, but rather a dabbing motion, dropping the paste onto the surface of the leaf. This will prevent disturbing the dried layers of paste underneath.

4. The third and forth coats of Paste Type should be a bit thicker consistency—more like a thin batter. Be sure to dry thoroughly between coats.

5. The fifth through tenth coats of Paste Type will be applied directly from the bottle. If the paste is too thick, add a few drops of water.

6. After the tenth coat, the leaf should have about 1mm coating of Paste Type. The leaf must feel substantial in your hand. Take a small amount of Art Clay Silver Clay and roll out a coil about 2mm thick and about 1" long.

7. Role the coil around the straw and let dry.

8. Add Paste Type to the coil and the front of the leaf and press into place. Secure the coil with additional Paste type and dry well. Remove the straw.

9. When ready to fire, place the leaf on a fiber blanket. This will help the leaf to keep its shape. Fire at 1600°F for 10 minutes. The leaf will burn away, leaving the silver.

10. When cool, remove the leaf, and brush with stainless steel brush.

11. File any sharp edges with a fine file.

12. Use a burnisher to highlight any raised areas. For an overall shine, use a rotary tumbler with stainless steel shot, water, and jewelry cleaner. Tumble for at least 1½ hours. Rinse and dry well. Add a chain to the finished piece.

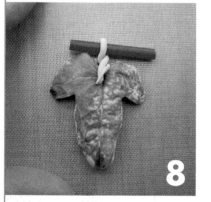

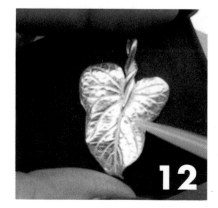

Basic Project

Syringe-made Bead & Pendant

Deb Jemmott

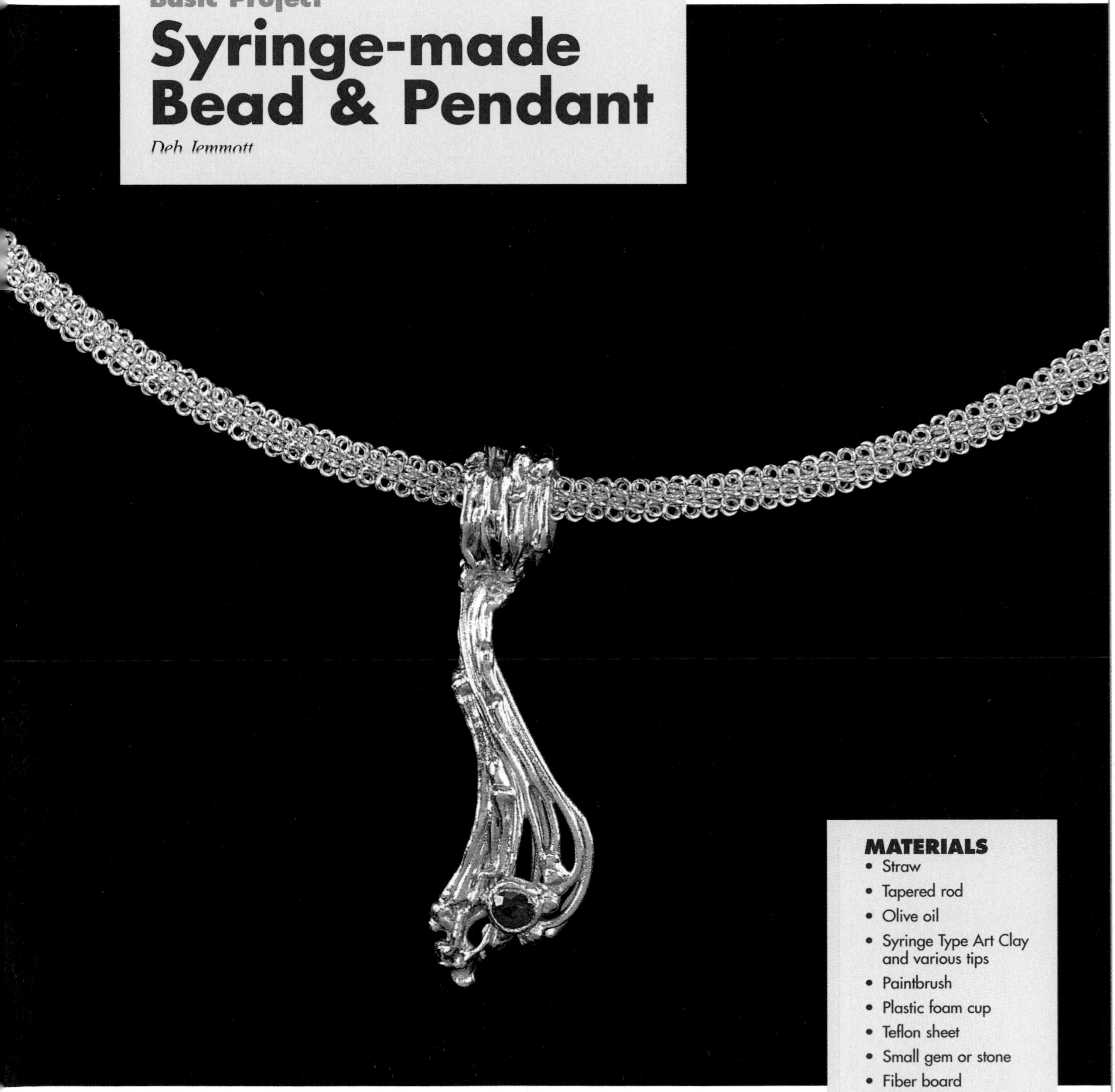

MATERIALS
- Straw
- Tapered rod
- Olive oil
- Syringe Type Art Clay and various tips
- Paintbrush
- Plastic foam cup
- Teflon sheet
- Small gem or stone
- Fiber board
- Craft knife

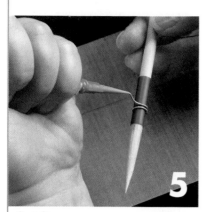

Part One

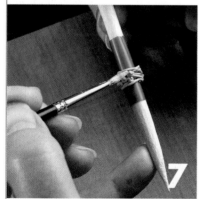

Part One

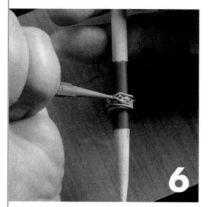

Part One

Part One

Part One

Instructions

1. Choose a straw with a slightly larger diameter than the desired finished bead or bail. (Remember the shrinkage.)

2. Cut the straw into pieces approximately 1" in length.

3. Find a tapered rod (a paintbrush, chopstick or an ink pen body) that the straw will slide on but then stop. This will enable you to spin the tapered rod to achieve the design without having to cut the straw after the design is complete.

4. Lightly grease the straw with olive oil.

5. Touch the syringe to the straw while pushing on the plunger.

6. Continue pushing the plunger, but bring the tip of the syringe slightly above the surface of the straw. Simultaneously, slowly spin the tapered rod so the syringe line will wrap around the straw. Touch the tip of the syringe to the straw when the line is complete. The lines may wrap completely or partially around the straw. Stagger the beginning and ending points of the syringe lines and layer the lines to create a more interesting effect. Using various tips on the syringe will result in different looks for the finished bead. The outside edge of the bead should have a double layer of syringe work.

7. If there are any sharp points or other flaws that develop, use a damp paintbrush to blend them.

8. Place the tapered rod so the syringe work can be suspended in the air to allow the syringe work to dry: Support the tapered rod on both ends (over a glass or small box). Alternatively, stab the end of the tapered rod into a piece of plasticene clay or floral foam, or a foam cup.

9. Once the syringe work is dry, remove the straw.

10. If the piece is particularly fragile, use a kiln prop inside the straw to support it. The kiln prop should be *loose* in the straw to allow for shrinkage of the clay.

11. After firing, the pieces may be brushed, tumbled, or worn to a natural burnish. If you are tumbling many beads, string them on a wire first, so they will be easy to remove from the tumbler.

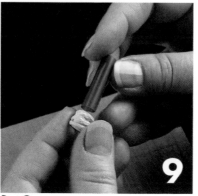

Part One

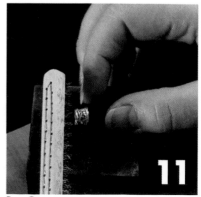

Part One

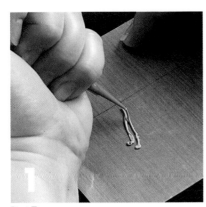

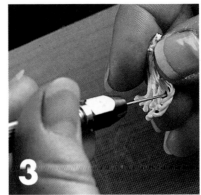

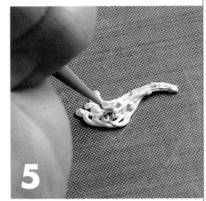

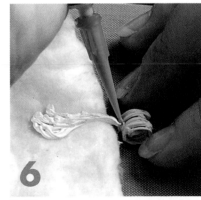

Part Two

A syringe bead may become a pendant bail by adding to it before or after the bead is fired. The pendant portion may be added directly to the dried bail, or made separately and added to the bail after drying, but before firing. Attaching the pendant to the bead is easier if the bail has not been fired, but is possible after firing. Allow the syringe work on the straw to dry completely before attempting to add to it.

Instructions

1. Working on a Teflex, non-stick sheet, use the syringe with a green tip to create overlapping lines, shaping into a mare's tail. Dry completely.

2. Once the pendant is dry, gently remove it from the baking sheet and turn it over. Work the back of the pendant with syringe in a corresponding manner to the front to give it dimension, strength, and interest. Dry completely.

3. Clean up the edges of the pendant with an emery board or file. Add smaller syringe work with a paintbrush to smooth it in.

4. Choose a stone and place the stone where it will go on the pendant. If it does not seat well, make a seat for it. Find a drill bit just smaller than the size of the stone. While supporting the piece from the back, gently spin the drill bit in your fingers to create a seat for the stone.

5. With the stone in place, work a syringe line around the outside of the stone. Two layers may be needed. The syringe must cover the girdle of the stone. Smooth with a damp paintbrush. Dry completely.

6. Prop the pendant part on a thin piece of fiber board in order to get it to the proper height to attach to the bail. Use paste and/or syringe to attach the pendant to the bail. Fill in any cracks or crevices and smooth with a damp paintbrush. Dry completely. Turn over and do the same on the back.

7. Before firing, make sure the stone is clean. Use a small file or craft knife to gently go around the stone to remove any excess clay and to clean any imperfections in the stone setting. A dry paintbrush will remove loose dust.

   If the syringe bead has already been fired: When adding to a bead, it's best that there is some "tooth" to it, so do not tumble the piece before adding anything. If the bead has been heavily tumbled and is very slick and shiny, it will be difficult to get the clay or additional syringe to stick to it. If the piece **has** been tumbled, use a scribe to put lines in the piece so it is not slick. For additional security, the pendant can be added on in such a way that the pieces interlock.

Which-came-first Filigree Egg

Judi Hendricks

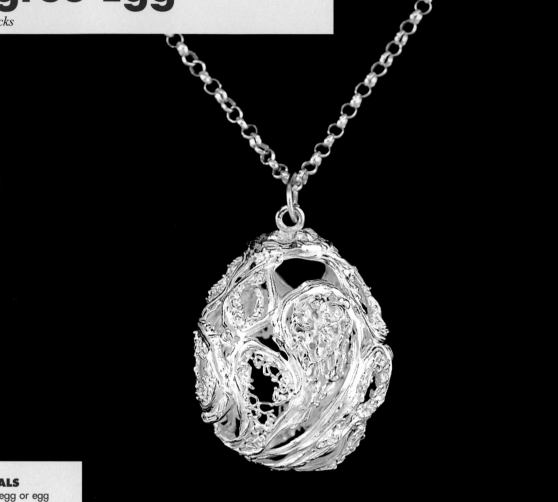

MATERIALS

- Hollow egg or egg form
- Fine-silver screw-eye
- Small amount of 22k gold clay paste
- 1 or 2 syringes of Art Clay silver, blue, green and cut green tip
- Plastic foam sheet
- Vinegar
- Toothpick
- Wire brush
- Craft knife

I suppose you could say that a friend egged me into doing this project—she has this Sun Conure bird that keeps laying eggs. She's a single mother (the bird, I mean), so the eggs aren't going to do anything interesting. My friend lets them dry out awhile and makes things out of them. When she offered one to me, I immediately hatched a scheme to turn it into a silver and gold filigree pendant.

Now you may be asking yourself, "Where can I get a tiny egg of my own to play with?" I have to be honest; unless you have a frisky pair of sparrows nesting on your windowsill (which, in point of fact, I do—and you'd be surprised how many "dud" eggs there are in a nesting season), or a hyper-reproductive canary, this could be a bit of a challenge. However, many Asian and specialty markets carry lovely little speckled quail eggs that aren't too eggs-pensive. You can blow the insides out through a pinhole in the top and bottom of the shell, cook it up and eat it like any other egg, leaving a tiny shell-form for an eggs-citing Art Clay project. Keep your eyes open in the spring for egg opportunities, but for goodness sake, keep your fingers off of those protected songbird eggs—and don't use plastic eggs, either; they produce toxic fumes when they burn).

Another suggestion is to make an egg-shaped form out of cork clay. But whatever base you use, always make sure it's bone-dry before kiln-firing it, or the trapped moisture will eggs-pand and the egg will eggs-huberantly eggs-plode.

Instructions

1. Depending upon your design and the size of your egg, this project will require one fine-silver screw-eye, a small amount of 22K gold clay paste, one or two syringes of Art Clay silver, a blue tip, a green tip, and a cut green tip. A cut green tip is exactly that (see project #14 in "Art Clay Silver"), a syringe tip that's had jagged slices cut into the tip with a craft knife. This creates a deliciously wavy texture in the extruded clay, and gives a perfect touch to *art nouveau* designs like the one I've used here. I mark my cut tips with a black "X" so I don't accidentally pick up the wrong syringe.

2. The secret to piping silver clay onto an egg is twofold: First, wipe the clay down with vinegar before you begin, rinse it off and let it dry well. The mild acid in the vinegar will "open" the porous surface of the egg so that the clay will cling better. Poke a hole in the bottom large enough to insert a toothpick to use as a "handle."

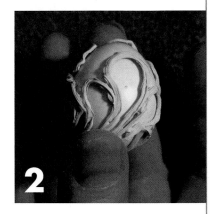

3. Secondly, whatever design you choose, make sure to "lock" all parts of the clay design together. That is to say, make sure that the main frame of your clay design goes all around the egg lengthwise and widthwise. If you don't lock the design together, when you dry the piece, the pieces will drop off of the egg, and probably distort while drying. Also, don't be shy—make sure that your main frame is relatively thick. You have to create a structure that will hold its shape during and after firing, and be strong enough to hold the weight of the filigree.

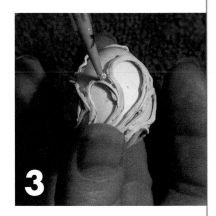

   In this design, I've used the cut green tip to create a series of swirling nested teardrops touching the top and bottom of the egg.

   Inserting the flat end of the toothpick into the egg, I jabbed the pointy-end of the toothpick into a flat-bottomed piece of plastic foam to hold the egg aloft in the dehydrator. Dry thoroughly so that you can handle it without smudging the design.

4. If you're a detail-oriented type of person who has to know where every little line is going to fall, this step is going to be hard for you. Pick the design detail that needs to be filled in with filigree silver and, using the blue syringe-tip, exert a fair amount of pressure on the plunger and allow the silver clay to tumble out in tiny, squiggly loops. (You may want to practice this on a piece of Teflex or some other non-stick surface before piping directly onto the egg. If your practice squiggles turn out well, you can always let them dry, then lift them with a paintbrush tip or craft knife and incorporate them into your egg design. If not, they can take a dive back into the paste jar.) Stack the loops up along the edges of the design detail and then move them out into the center of the area. Let this layer of clay dry thoroughly, and check for thin spots. If the design looks thin, squiggle on some more

and tap it down lightly, while wet, to ensure good adhesion to the previous layer. In my design I "closed" some of the filigree teardrops by filling in the centers and left others open.

5. There would be several ways to attach a jump ring to the egg pendant; the way I chose was to pipe a ring of clay around the top and place a small round piece of clay that had been rubber-stamped with a tiny flower over it, like a cap. Then I eased a fine silver screw-eye into the clay. After the clay has set enough to hold the screw-eye, use the green syringe tip to touch up the neck of the screw-eye, making sure it's securely captured. Dry thoroughly.

6. I poached an idea from Jackie (you have no idea how many chicken/egg puns there are—I've really shown remarkable restraint!) and added a gold vermeil layer to two of the filigree windows. It's a lovely and ineggs-pensive touch. Using 22k gold clay paste (made by mixing a gram of gold clay with a few drops of water), brush three layers of gold clay over a select area, letting it dry thoroughly between coats. Be sure to paint the gold paste around the edges of the filigree so that as it fires it will drip down onto the coils and loops.

7. Make sure you "snug" your egg into position on a fiber blanket when firing so that it doesn't roll while sintering. Remember to make sure your item and supporting substructure form—be it egg shell or clay—are thoroughly dry before firing to avoid vapor explosions. And, if using a cork clay "egg" form, remember to follow Art Clay safety and firing directions: No peeking at cork clay while it's in the kiln or the introduction of oxygen into the anaerobic chamber could cause your piece to burst into flame and superheat, damaging and possibly destroying your piece. Fire at 1472°F for 30 minutes.

8. Notice how the eggshell kept its shape in the fired piece? Even after firing, the eggshell was so firm that I had to poke through it in several places with a micro-file to break it apart. As soon as I'd broken through the shell under running water, however, it quickly began to dissolve.

9. I lightly (and I mean *lightly!*) brushed the fired piece with a wire brush to remove the powdery white coating, but after that I put it into a tumbler with stainless-steel shot and tumbling solution and let it polish for a couple of hours. I've always had extremely good luck shot-tumbling delicate pieces—much better luck than trying to brush or sand them—yet I know designers who have had pieces seriously damaged by shot-tumbling. I suspect that this is because I use a small, low-power, rubber-barrel type tumbler; my guess is that some of the larger, hardier tumblers may be too robust for this type of polishing. You'll have to experiment with this for yourself and find which finishing method gives you the best results.

10. On my little egg, the results were even better than I'd hoped; it's a lovely, light-weight pendant with lots of sparkle and gold shine. When I showed my friend the finished piece, she liked it so much she gave me another egg.

To which I say: "Eggs-cellent!"

Basic Project
Freeform Soft-fold Torn Pendant

Jonna Faulkner
Steve Rossman, photographs

MATERIALS
- 1 package Art Clay Silver Sheet Type, 10g (or Regular Clay type, rolled 1mm thick)
- Small amount of Art Clay Silver Paste
- 20-gauge fine silver wire, 2"
- Pearls, half-drilled, 2
- Scissors
- Paintbrush with a small, pointed tip
- Water
- Olive oil
- Plastic wrap
- Toothpicks and straws to use as props as needed
- Wet/dry sandpaper, 600 grit
- Small metal files
- Cosmetic sponge pieces
- Hairdryer
- Programmable kiln
- Fiber board kiln shelf
- Fiber blanket
- Wire brush
- Wire cutters
- Chain or flat nose pliers
- Fine point black marker
- Clear epoxy to attach pearls
- Thin straw
- Toothpick

Although this project can be done by rolling out Regular Clay to the desired thickness, why bother when Sheet Type does it for you? Sure it's lazy, sure it's indulgent. But why not treat yourself? Besides, you can't beat the smooth, satiny finish!

Instructions

1. Before beginning work, make sure you have assembled all tools and materials for this project.

2. Open the package containing the Art Clay Silver Sheet type.

3. Peel off both sheets of protective plastic from Sheet Type clay.

4. Tear off opposite corners of Sheet Type clay.

5. Place main body of Sheet Type on work surface. Place small, torn pieces on plastic wrap. Use brush to lightly moisten these pieces with water.

   Fold up plastic wrap so these pieces stay flat and retain moisture. Reserve these pieces to make the bail (and a platform for the bail, if necessary).

6. Lubricate fingers very lightly with olive oil.

7. Use fingers to manipulate clay and shape pendant.

   Take advantage of the Sheet Type's fabric-like malleability to create soft folds and curved surfaces. Prop up selected areas with straws or toothpicks as desired. Make sure the torn edges show in the design to emphasize the contrast between smooth surfaces and rough edges.

8. When you have formed a pleasing shape, decide on its top-and-bottom orientation. Then guide the fine silver wire through the soft folds of the piece. You'll find that you can pierce the sheet clay easily with the wire. Don't move the wire in such a way as to create large holes as it travels through the clay.

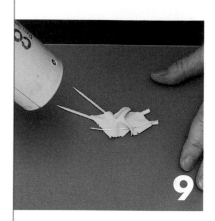

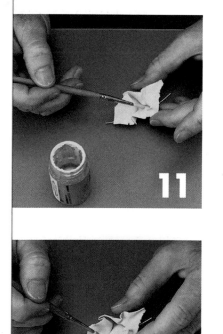

9. Dry the piece with the hairdryer. Be careful not to get the hairdryer too close to the piece if you have used plastic straws as props because the heat could melt them.

10. Once the pendant is dry enough to lift off the work surface, turn it over and dry its back.

11. The next step will lock the silver wire in place. Use your brush to apply paste at each place on the back of the pendant where the wire enters and exits the clay.

    Dry and repeat several times to build up a thick body of paste to capture the wire. If folds in the clay conceal some entry/exit points, do not worry. As long as at least one entry and exit point are thoroughly surrounded by paste, the wire will be held securely once your piece has been fired. Dry.

12. Apply paste to back to reinforce torn edges as needed. Dry.

13. The next steps will create a hidden bail. Check the final "look" of your pendant before beginning work on the bail by placing a thin straw on your work surface. Then place your piece on the straw, front side up, so that the straw ends protrude beyond the sides of the pendant. This will show you the path your stringing material will travel on either side of your pendant. Generally, the bail should be placed so that most of the pendant hangs below its pathway.

14. Turn the piece over and examine the area on the back where you've determined the bail would best be positioned. You may be lucky and have sufficient contact points on the back to proceed to making the bail. Most likely, however, you will need to create a platform on which the bail can rest.

15. Prop your piece so that the back is level. Open the plastic wrap in which you placed the torn corners of Sheet Type. You will use these pieces to create your bail platform and the bail. Select one corner, reserving the remainder for the bail itself. Lightly moisten the remainder again before folding it back into the plastic wrap.

16. Lightly moisten the small piece on your work surface. Determine how it can be cut and pasted together across the back of your piece to create a flat platform for the bail.

17. Paste the piece of the bail platform to the back of the pendant. In this case, the first section of the bail platform protrudes beyond the top of the pendant to complete the design as a whole.

18. Create the flattest possible surface for the bail. Paste all joins and dry. If needed, sand the surface of the bail platform to make it level. Apply paste across the whole surface of the bail platform and dry.

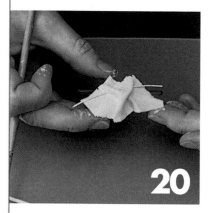

19. Open the plastic wrap and take out the remaining piece of clay. Moisten lightly to maintain its pliability. In most instances, this piece of clay will be triangular in shape. Paint the longest side of the triangle with paste. Paint the bail platform with paste, and then place the triangle on the bail platform with the tip of the triangle aimed to the top of the pendant. Place a small straw on the portion of the triangle on the bail platform. Bring the tip of the triangle down so that it curves around the straw. Paint the inner surface of the tip of the triangle with paste and attach it either to the underside of the bail platform or to the pendant back if the triangle will reach that far. Use a toothpick to help set this bail end in place. Gently pick up the pendant. Check the front of the piece to see where the ends of the straw emerge from its sides. Be sure that the pathway indicated by the straw ends will be appropriate for your stringing material. Dry.

20. When the piece is dry enough that the straw will turn easily in the bail, gently remove the straw and dry the interior of the bail. Check your piece and add paste to any joins of the bail that need reinforcement. Dry the piece completely.

21. Examine the piece for rough spots and gently file off any sharp points.

22. Set the piece, face up, on the fiber blanket so the bail will not distort during firing. Fire at 1600°F for 10 minutes.

23. After the piece has been fired and cooled, brush vigorously with the stainless steel brush.

   Check again for sharp areas and file as necessary.

24. There are a variety of finishes that would work well for this pendant. I like the lustrous satin finish created by brushing this pendant, so I don't patina or tumble it.

25. Mounting the pearls is the final step, no matter which finish you choose. First, you need to work-harden the fine silver wire. To do this, grasp one end of the wire with chain nose or flat nose pliers. Hold the piece steady in your other hand and pull on the wire.

   You will be able to see and feel it stretch a little. Repeat this process with the other end of the wire.

26. The tips of the wire will have flattened during the stretching process so they probably will no longer fit into the pearl. To correct this problem, clip the very tips of the wire with your wire cutters. Insert one end of the wire into the pearl. Use your black marker to mark the wire at the place where the pearl stops. Remove the pearl. Measure the wire from its tip to the mark. This will tell you how deep the drill hole of the pearl is. It's best to cut the wire so that most of the pearl rests on the pendant, primarily because the fine silver wire will hold its shape and position in short lengths but will tend to bend easily if left too long.

27. Place the other pearl on the other end of the wire and repeat the process of marking and cutting.

28. Use a clear epoxy to glue the pearl to the wire. Follow the directions on the epoxy for mixing and drying. On the span of the wire that will fit into the pearl, gently file two small lines to give the wire "tooth" so that the glue will bond the wire to the pearl more easily. Try not to flatten or distort the tip of the wire while making the lines. Check to make sure that the wire will still fit into the pearl. Apply the glue to the wire with a toothpick. Insert the wire into the pearl. A collar of glue will form around the exterior of the pearl where it meets the wire. Clean that carefully with toothpicks so that no glue remains on the outside of the pearl. Allow the glue to set for the length of time specified on the directions.

Mesh Screen Pendant

Jonna Faulkner
Steve Rossman, photographs

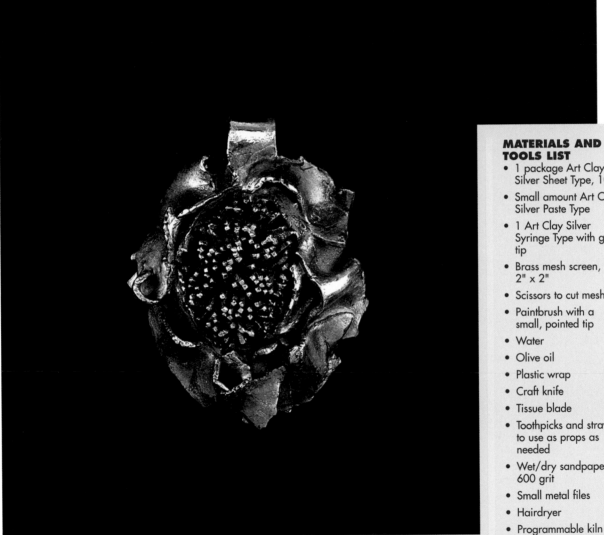

MATERIALS AND TOOLS LIST

- 1 package Art Clay Silver Sheet Type, 10g
- Small amount Art Clay Silver Paste Type
- 1 Art Clay Silver Syringe Type with gray tip
- Brass mesh screen, 2" x 2"
- Scissors to cut mesh
- Paintbrush with a small, pointed tip
- Water
- Olive oil
- Plastic wrap
- Craft knife
- Tissue blade
- Toothpicks and straws to use as props as needed
- Wet/dry sandpaper, 600 grit
- Small metal files
- Hairdryer
- Programmable kiln
- Fiberboard kiln shelf
- Kiln soft fiber blanket
- Stainless-steel brush
- Black marker
- Liver of Sulfur
- Nail polish remover
- Small, dedicated measuring cup for nail polish remover
- Cotton cosmetic pads
- Agate knife or other burnishing tool

Using brass mesh is one of my favorite design tricks. It is also what makes this an advanced project. It takes a little practice to be able to get the extruded clay through the mesh without flattening or otherwise destroying it's shape. And, though there are certainly other mesh metals out there, such as bronze and copper, we strongly suggest you stick with brass, which is more stable during firing.

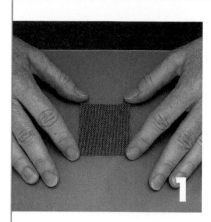

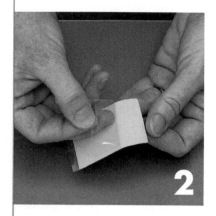

Instructions

1. Before opening your clay, assemble all tools and materials required for this project. Make sure your piece of brass mesh is at least 2" x 2" for a first attempt at this technique.

2. Open Art Clay Silver Sheet Type. You will find that the clay is encased in two sheets of plastic. Roll the top sheet of plastic back just enough to uncover about one quarter of the clay.

3. Use your craft knife to cut a small ½" long oval shape in the clay. Remove the oval shape. Use this shape as a template to cut two more same size oval shapes. Cut a small piece of scrap from this area of the clay.

4. Lightly moisten the three ovals and piece of scrap as well as the exposed clay on the plastic sheet. Roll the plastic sheet back over the remainder of the Sheet Type and place the whole on plastic wrap. Fold the plastic wrap around the Sheet Type to keep it moist and pliable for later use.

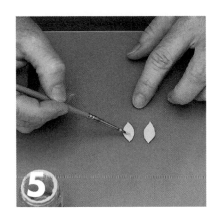

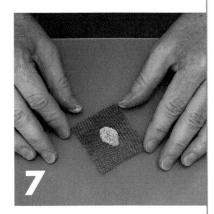

5. Apply paste with brush to each oval and stack them on top of each other. Paint the small piece of scrap with paste and place in on the middle of the stack of ovals.

6. Place the stack of ovals and scrap on the middle of the piece of mesh. Place your thumbs on the clay and your fingers on the outer margins of the front of the screen. Tilt the screen toward you and push the clay through the screen. Depending on the size of the mesh, you may have to push quite hard. The mesh will dome while you perform this operation. This is a desirable effect. Be careful not to get your fingers on the clay that comes through the screen as that can mar the extrusions. Leave some clay on the back surface so that the screen will be captured between the front extrusions and the clay on the back when fired.

7. At this point, your mesh may have acquired a sharp u-shape. Set the screen on your work surface, dome-side up, and gently push the margins of the mesh down so that the dome remains but the "u" is gone.

8. Dry the clay, front and back.

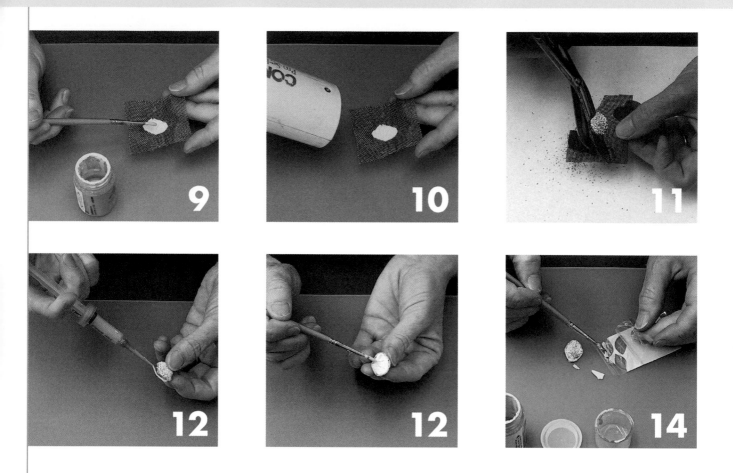

9. Apply two layers of paste to the clay on the back of the screen. Dry between each coat.

10. Make sure that the piece is completely dry. Place on the kiln shelf and fire at 1472°F for 30 minutes. This will sinter the Art Clay without melting or weakening the brass.

11. Allow the piece to cool. The mesh will be black and heavily oxidized. Working over a sheet of disposable paper or a wastebasket, cut the extraneous mesh away from the fired clay oval. (The mesh captured in the oval will remain in the piece.) Throw away the disposable paper and cut pieces of mesh. If any bit of wire or oxidation gets on your work surface, be sure to remove it before continuing to build this pendant.

12. Grasp the middle of the oval and surround its edges with Art Clay Silver Syringe Type extruded from the gray tip. Let the syringe extrusion dry slightly and then lightly pat it onto the oval so as to cover any little bits of wire that may be poking out. Dry completely.

13. Fix the syringe work in place by applying paste to the entire back of the piece. Dry completely. Apply a second coat of paste if necessary. Dry again.

14. Remove the remainder of the Sheet Type from the plastic wrap. Roll the top sheet of plastic back just enough to tear off a fragment of Sheet Type. Lightly moisten and re-cover the remainder of the Sheet Type. Apply paste to the fragment and place it on the edge of the oval. Lift the fragment, apply paste to the desired spot on the oval, and replace the fragment.

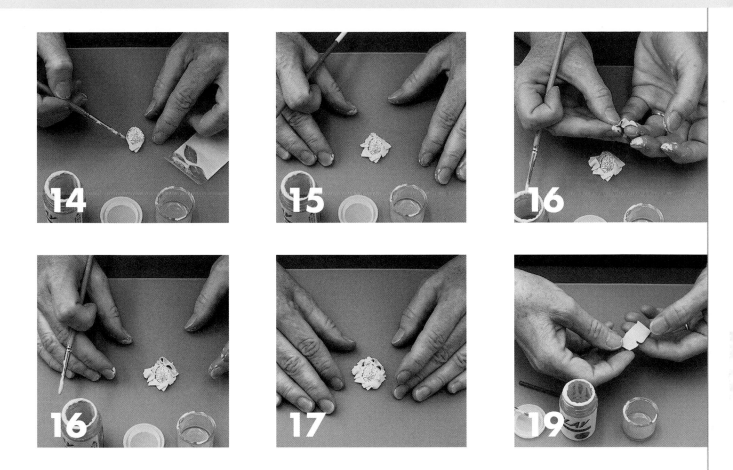

15. Repeat these steps until you've enclosed the frame with fragments. Since this is a free-form piece, you can cover as much or as little of the oval as you like.

16. The next steps will finish the frame. Tear a ribbon-shaped strip off the remainder of the Sheet Type. Fold, roll, or curve it in ways that are pleasing to your eye. Place it on the frame, pasting each contact point. Use straws or toothpicks as props for ripples or other three-dimensional effects as necessary. Be sure to leave enough Sheet Type in the plastic wrap cocoon to allow for the creation of a bail and for a bit more decoration once the bail is in place.

17. Repeat these steps until you have decorated the frame to your satisfaction. Dry the piece completely.

18. Turn the piece over and apply paste to all joins. Dry.

19. Open the Sheet Type again and tear off a strip long and wide enough to create a bail.

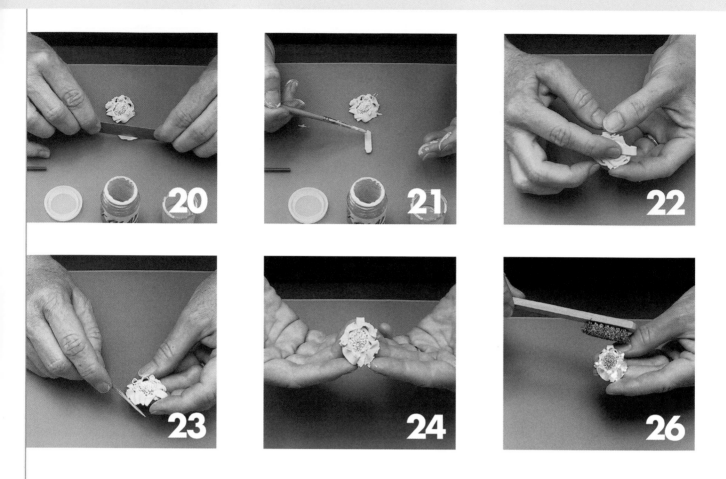

20. Trim the sides of the bail with a tissue blade if a clean edge is desired.

21. Apply paste to one end of the bail and to the upper back of the pendant. Place the pendant, right side up, on the pasted end of the bail. Place a straw of suitable diameter for the piece on the bail next to the top of the pendant. Lift the exposed end of the bail up, bring it around the straw and paste this end to the front of the pendant.

22. Dry enough so you can lift up the piece. The end of the bail on the back of the pendant may need to be pasted and pushed in so it rests against the back of the piece. Dry completely.

23. Check piece for sharp edges and points. Smooth with file as needed.

24. Examine the front of the piece for design and balance. Make sure the pendant is completely dry.

25. Place the piece on kiln blanket on the kiln shelf. Fire the pendant at 1472°F for 30 minutes.

26. Allow the pendant to cool. Brush the piece with a stainless steel brush.

27. If desired, add patina to your piece. Start this process by applying black marker to areas on the pendant where you'd like to retain a bright-silver look. The marker acts as a resist to the Liver of Sulfur patina solution. Then quickly dip and remove the piece from the hot Liver of Sulfur bath, and immediately rinse it off in cold water. Repeat these steps until you're happy with the colors created by the patina solution.

28. Select a small glass or plastic measuring cup with a pour spout for the next step. Put the piece in the cup and cover the pendant with nail polish remover. The nail polish remover acts as a solvent for the mark. Use a disposable cotton pad to aid in the clean-up process. Rinse the piece in clear water. Pour the remaining nail polish remover back into its bottle for future use.

29. Burnish the edges and other areas of the piece with an agate knife or other burnishing tool as desired.

30. The color and degree of patination vary with each piece; they are affected by the warmth and strength of the Liver of Sulfur solution, the time spent in the solution with each dip, the amount of brushing and burnishing before dipping, and the way your luck is going on that day. You can always re-fire the piece in the kiln to remove the patination and start the process over again if you're not happy the first time around.

Take it Slow (Slow Dry, That Is)

Basic Project

Summer Roses

Leighton Taylor

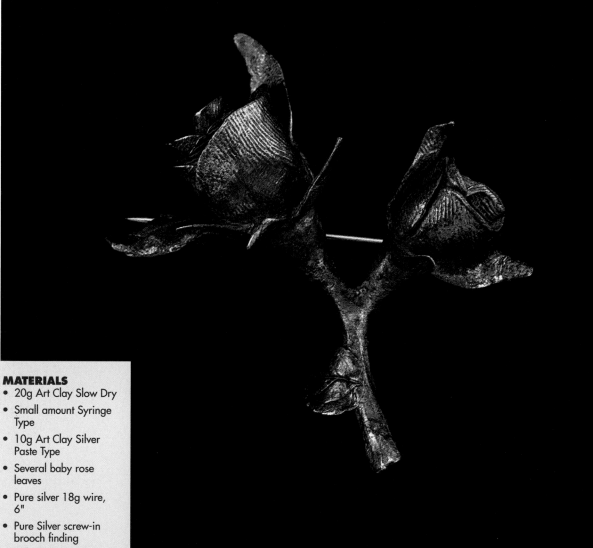

MATERIALS

- 20g Art Clay Slow Dry
- Small amount Syringe Type
- 10g Art Clay Silver Paste Type
- Several baby rose leaves
- Pure silver 18g wire, 6"
- Pure Silver screw-in brooch finding
- Plastic re-sealable bags
- Olive oil
- Files
- 600, 1200, and 2000 grit sandpaper
- Liver of Sulfur
- 1.5mm drill bit
- Pin vise
- 3 - 4 leaves
- Craft knife

This Summer Rose is a perfect Slow Dry beginning project. The clay gives you plenty of time to design and place your roses, and the petals don't have to be exact or perfect, since every rose is different!

Instructions

1. Assemble various tools as required.

2. Assemble pin back according to directions and set aside. Make sure "nuts" are clean by washing with soap and water and patting dry.

3. Remove the Slow Dry from the package and knead in your hands. The clay will quickly soften as it warms. Use a drop of olive oil on tools and hands to prevent sticking. I always start from a nice round smooth ball, and recondition by adding water if necessary.

4. Divide your clay in three, and put two-thirds back into plastic re-sealable bags.

5. Pinch ball off, and make it approximately half the size of a pea. Cup remaining clay in other hand to keep warm. If this is your first time working with Slow Dry, you might consider dividing the clay up into balls and then put the ones you are not working on in a plastic re-sealable bag. This will give you more time to focus on each ball.

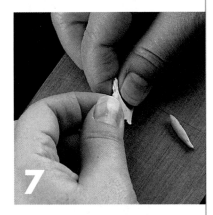

6. Flatten ball into a round disc for petals. With practice, you'll pinch and flatten at the same time. The fingerprints add great texture and ideally you will want the edges very thin. The goal is the appearance of delicate petals and leaves.

7. Roll up the first petal to form the core petal. Repeat creation of clay disc, and begin overlapping the petals. Don't stop until you have five or six petals. Use paste sparingly at the base to hold pieces together, and pinch the base to get the petals to stick together. Spin the flattened disc around until you get the edge that best matches a petal. Individually, the discs may not be very special or nice, but in a group you will get surprisingly good results, so press on if you have trouble with an individual petal. No one will notice minor variations.

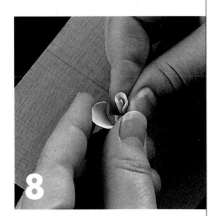

8. Once attached to the core, the petals may be shaped, and you may close the flower, or open the petals. Slow dry should give you enough time to make these minor alterations without cracking the clay. If you find resistance, don't force it, just remoisten, and allow the clay to become pliable again. The base can remain rough as it will be covered by the stem and leaves later.

9. Once you have several petals, you may stop and keep this small rose, or continue using progressively larger petals. Don't use more than half your clay on your main rose. Once the flower petals are together, apply paste to the base, and then create a small stem for the rose that covers and cements the bottom of the flower together. Dry.

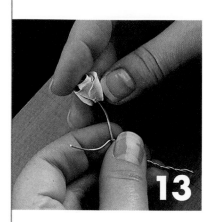

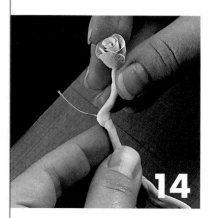

10. Repeat petal process, for second rose. Make it slightly smaller than the first, and store remaining clay for later.

11. Cut the 18g wire in half, and twist together half way up. Set aside. I make the wire assembly larger than necessary, as it is much easier to remove than add.

12. Making the opened bud leaves around the rose is similar to making the petals, except you start with a pointed cone, and then flatten the cone. Fingerprints accent the leaves. Bending or twisting the leaves produces nice effects. Attach to the bud using paste, and arrange the layout to accent the flower. Remember, the flowers will have a back, and the back should be flat so the piece will hang nicely. The leaves should not stick straight out, and allow room for the other flower. The leaves should be attached to the base with a bulb of clay, which mimics a real rose. Use paste to ensure good joints. Go immediately to the next step, and do not let work completely dry.

13. Impale the flowers on the ends of the wires; bury wire at least one-quarter of the way into the flower. Using needle nose pliers, bend wire into an appealing arrangement. Use props to keep flowers in the desired position.

14. Wrap the wire in clay, leaving the twisted end sticking out of the clay. This is important as it allows for clay shrinkage. Use paste to ensure a good bond between the flowers and stem, and fill any large cracks with Syringe Type. Dry thoroughly.

15. Clean up stem with files and 600 grit sandpaper before adding leaves. The petals and leaves should not require any sanding.

16. The secret behind good leaves? Use real leaves, apply paste to the underside, as it has more pronounced veins. Use two thick, even coats, allowing clay to dry between applications. Remember, they are supposed to be delicate and thin. Do not fire them.

17. Attach leaves to the stem using paste; offsetting the smaller flower makes for a nice arrangement.

18. Dry work, file, and sand stem. The stem should be sturdy, so let it remain somewhat thick.

19. The brooch findings can be arranged on the back of the piece and, if necessary, you may trim the pin so that it is shorter. The screw in "nuts" will be fired in with the Art Clay, and the pin and catch will be screwed off immediately before firing, but not before.

20. Prepare the smaller flower brooch mount by wetting the dried clay area with water. Make sure that you are far enough down the flower that your work will not be visible from the front. Wetting the area makes it easier to drill the hole in back of the flowers for the brooch finding, and helps prevent cracking. Setting the brooch high into the flowers allows the piece to hang more upright, and not tilt forward. Don't drill too far, between a third and half of the height of the finding. Use light pressure on the pin vise and let the drill bit do the work. Remove excess clay filings and recycle. Enlarge the hole with a craft knife or file.

21. Anchor the brooch finding with Syringe Type, similar to the process for setting a lab created stone. Ensure that the pin catch lines up with where the pin will be. Apply two coils of Syringe Type, and then press in the setting. Let dry, then take care to scrape off any clay that may have attached itself to the screw or the catch, as these need to be able to come easily on and off. Clean and fill in the edges of the hole, and remember the clay will shrink, so the screw part of the catch must have room on all sides down to the nut.

22. The pin is anchored to the underside of a leaf. A small piece of clay is wrapped around the edges of the finding, which is then attached and built up with syringe. The pin is lined up with the catch before using the syringe to glue it to the leaf. Syringe work covers underneath the pin finding as well.

23. Take care that the pin can screw in and out, and once again account for possible shrinkage around screw.

24. Dry and finish cleaning up the stem and finding. Wire should still emerge from the end of the rose to allow for shrinkage. Very carefully support the setting as you unscrew the pin and catch. Fire at 1600°F. for 10 minutes. Cool.

25. Trim protruding wire, file end. Brush with stainless steel brush and polish with wet 600 and 1200 grit sandpaper.

26. Patina in Liver of Sulfur to highlight edges, and darken recesses. (See Patina, page 39.)

27. Finish piece by screwing in clutch and pin findings. Secure with a drop of epoxy, making sure not to glue pin hinge or clutch locking mechanism.

Silver Braided Ring

Text by Patricia Walton

MATERIALS

- 10 gms Slow Dry Art Clay Silver
- Small amount Paste Type
- Fine silver, 5mm round, 4-prong setting
- 5mm round faceted stone
- Teflon® coated work surface
- Teflex® strip
- Empty syringe
- Craft knife
- Paper clip
- Small paintbrush
- Ring sizer
- Ring mandrel
- Butane torch
- Firing brick
- Tweezers
- Stainless steel wire brush
- Burnisher
- Rawhide mallet
- Cosmetic sponge
- 600, 1200, and 2000 grit wet/dry sandpaper
- Hairdryer or food dehydrator
- Jewelry pliers
- Wenol metal polish
- Olive oil
- Rubber block

One of the most unique characteristics of Art Clay Slow Dry clay is its ability to be manipulated into complex shapes without drying, cracking or breaking. This braided ring shows Slow Dry to its best advantage. Try braiding with regular Art Clay and you'll see what we mean!

Instructions

1. Determine your ring size by finding the ring sizer that fits the finger your ring will be worn on. Then, choose the ring sizer that is 1½ sizes larger. (For example, if your finger measures a size 8, make the ring a 9½.) The additional size will compensate for the approximate 10 percent shrinkage that occurs when the binder and water burn off.

2. Roll up a Teflex strip approximately 1½" wide and tape it closed so it can slip inside the appropriate larger ring sizer. Next, slide the strip onto the ring mandrel. The appropriate sized ring sizer is then slipped on over the Teflex strip. With both the Teflex strip and ring sizer in place on the mandrel, draw a pencil mark all the way around the ring sizer along both edges onto the Teflex form. These marks will act as guides when making the ring. Now you can remove the ring sizer, leaving the correct ring size marking in pencil on the Teflex strip.

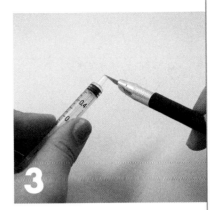

3. The opening at the end of the syringe should be about 2mm. If the syringe opening is too small, cut about 1mm off the end with a craft knife to create a larger opening. You are now ready to open the 10 grams of Art Clay Slow Dry.

4. Divide the clay in half and store one half in a small, air-tight container for later use. Slow Dry clay needs to be kneaded with your fingers until soft and warm before you can use it. Knead the clay, then hand-form a rope that is small enough to fit easily into the empty syringe.

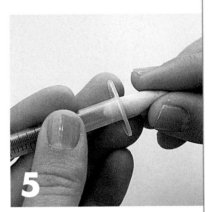

5. Remove the syringe plunger. Place the straightened end of a paper clip into the tip of the syringe and add the rope of clay. Replace the plunger and slowly depress to compress the clay in the syringe. The presence of the paper clip will prevent any air pockets from forming. Remove the clip when the clay begins to extrude through the opening. Tip: Always keep the tip of the filled syringe in a container of water when not in use. This will prevent air from drying the clay while it is in the syringe. Once the project is complete, remove any leftover clay and clean the syringe.

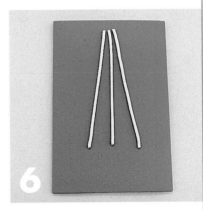

6. You will need five extruded ropes, three for the braiding and two to attach to the edges of the ring. I advise extruding only the three for braiding at this point. Press the plunger slowly and extrude three equal ropes, side by side, onto a non-stick work surface. To create a ring up to a size 6, 4" to 5" ropes will be sufficient. For each additional half size, add 2mm to the length of each rope. Return the syringe to the container of water.

7. Moisten the extruded ropes with a damp brush. Braid to the end, keeping the ropes damp as you go. Secure the ends by pressing with your finger or sculpting tool to flatten the last ⅛" of the braid. Add paste to keep the ends together if needed.

8. Dampen the braid and transfer it to the ring mandrel, positioning it over the pencil marks on the Teflex sheet. Let the ends overlap and, using a craft knife, cut on an angle across the braid. Remove the excess. Line up the ends and join using the paste applied with a brush. Place the excess clay in the airtight container for later use.

9. Using tweezers, place the fine silver, 5mm setting over the joint area. The setting should be pressed into the wet clay up to the second "wire." Add paste, if needed, to fill the area up to the second wire, securing the setting in place. Leaving the ring on the mandrel, dry it using a hairdryer or dehydrator for at least 15 minutes. The clay will turn a lighter gray when dry—Slow Dry takes five times longer to dry than regular Art Clay.

10. When dry, extrude two more ropes using the remaining Slow Dry in the syringe. Attach one rope to each side of the braid using paste applied with a small brush. Cut the ends of the ropes at an angle and join each on the back of the ring, opposite the 5mm stone setting. Add paste to fill in any gaps between the braids and the ropes. Dry again until the added ropes are completely dry.

11. Remove the Teflex sheet and the ring from the mandrel. Carefully remove the Teflex sheet from the inside of the ring. If it sticks, dry the ring off of the mandrel for a few more minutes. Once the Teflex is removed from inside the ring, check all contact points on the inside and outside of the ring, adding paste to fill in any gaps or cracks. Dry completely before refining.

12. Refine the ring by filing with small files and sanding using 600 and 1200 grit dry sandpaper. All seams and joints should be invisible. Save all the filings as they can be added to your paste jar. You can further perfect your ring by smoothing with a wet wipe or damp makeup sponge. Let dry again.

13. Once you are pleased with your final clay shape, you are ready to fire your creation using a small hand-held butane torch. Since there are many torch brands available, be sure to read the instructions included with your torch on filling the torch with fuel, igniting it, and flame adjustment. Firing should be done in a well-ventilated area clear of any flammable materials.

14. Place the ring on a firing block. Have a timer or watch with a second hand available to time the sintering. Light the torch and direct the end of the flame about 1" from the ring. The flame should be directed at a 45 degree angle and kept moving in a circle around the ring. The ring will begin to smoke and flame for a few seconds as the non-toxic binder burns away. The larger the piece, the more smoke and flame will occur. You can successfully fire clay creations that weigh less than 26 grams and have an area smaller than the size of a silver dollar. Continue to circle the ring until it begins to glow orange—dimming or turning out the lights will make it easier to see the glow. The color you are watching for is the same one metalsmiths use for annealing metal. Adjust the distance and speed of circling to maintain that rosy/peach color for 2 minutes. Timing begins only after the orange glow is achieved. During the firing time, the micro particles of the clay sinter to create a solid ring. After 2 minutes, turn off the torch and allow the ring to cool. Using metal tweezers, you can place the ring on a metal surface to help draw off the heat, or use the cool setting on a hairdryer to help bring the temperature down.

15. To finish the ring, support it on a rubber block and brush with a stainless steel fine wire brush. The silver will become noticeable immediately and will have a satin finish. You can stop at this point, or you can continue by highlighting areas with a polished steel burnisher. If you filed, sanded, and smoothed your ring in the clay state, very little effort will be needed to finish the ring. If you want to take the finishing process further, you can sand the ring using dampened wet/dry 600, 1200, and 2000 grit sandpaper to create a mirror finish, metal polish such as Wenol on a soft cloth to achieve a high polish—or use any traditional metalsmithing finishing techniques including tumble finishing.

16. If your ring is not round, place on a steel ring mandrel and tap lightly using a rawhide mallet, being careful to avoid the four-prong setting.

17. The four-prong setting has a small notch near the top and on the inside of each prong as a seat for the girdle of the stone. Place the stone into the setting. Adjust the prongs using pliers or tweezers until the stone sits perfectly in the notches. Secure the stone by placing fine-point half round or flat nose pliers on opposing prongs. Slightly rock the pliers back and forth until the tips begin to lie over the girdle of the stone. Place one face of the pliers under the edge of the ring and the other face on the prong and gently press the prong onto the face of the stone. Work on opposite prongs until all four prongs are tightened. Check to make sure the stone will not move in the setting and that the stone is level. Place the ring onto the mandrel and carefully burnish the tips smooth. Your ring is now ready to show off, wear, and enjoy.

Advanced Project
Fanfolded Earrings
Jackie Truty

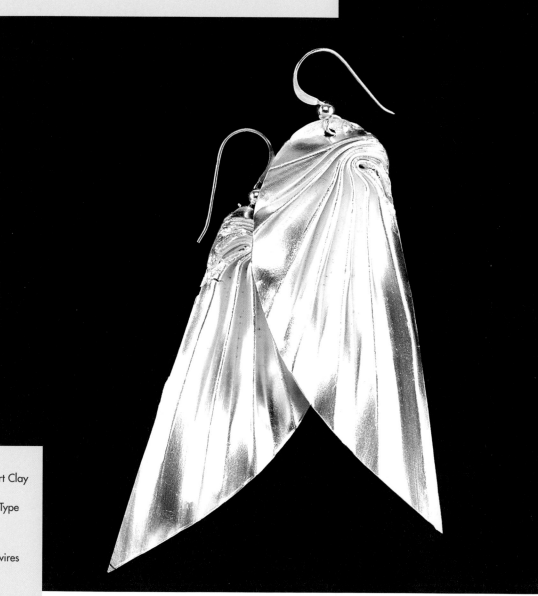

MATERIALS
- 10gm Paper Type Art Clay Silver
- Small amount Paste Type
- Craft knife
- Ruler
- Sterling French ear wires
- Pliers
- Pencil
- Paintbrush
- Pin vise
- 1.5mm drill bit
- Teflon-coated work surface
- Mini power tool
- Stainless wire wheel
- Small file
- Fiber blanket

What makes this project advanced is not the design; that's relatively simple. It's the difficulty in keeping the folds together long enough to complete the project without adding too much moisture or too much heat. Once you've got the techniques of handling Paper Type down, it's a blast to use!

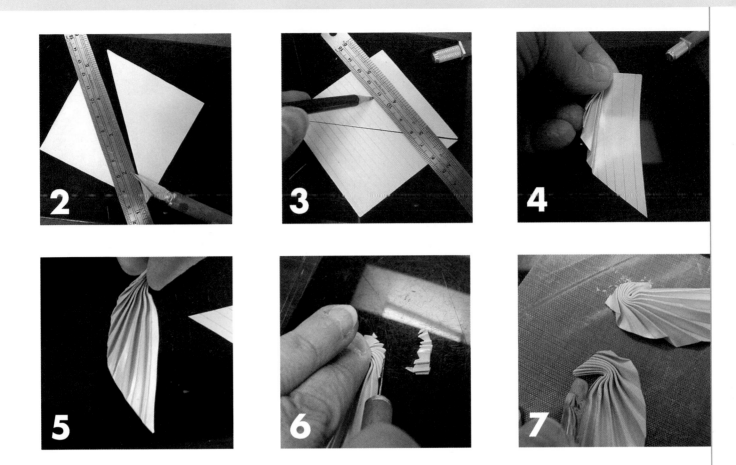

Instructions

1. Unwrap the package of Paper Type and place on the Teflon working surface.

2. Laying the ruler diagonally, cut the Paper Type square into two equal triangles.

3. Using the ruler and a pencil, begin drawing a very light line every $1/8$" or so, beginning parallel to one side.

4. Starting at the shortest pointed side, begin folding the triangle, accordion style. Make certain you press each fold firmly, creasing deeply.

5. Carefully gather the folds up and hold by the pointed end.

6. Lay the folded triangle on end on a flat surface and bend the gathered folds toward the long end. With a craft knife, cut the excess Paper Type off of the curve so that there is a straight line from the longest point up to the curve.

7. Holding the folds together, paint a small amount of Paste Type between and around the folds. Hold for a minute or so until the bend stays in place. Again using the craft knife, reshape the top point so that it is rounded. This will be the location of the hole for the French wires.

8. Take the paintbrush and put a thick layer of Paste Type on the raw ends of the fold, being careful not to let the Paste Type drip onto the sides of the folds. Any moisture allowed to touch the sides will not only ruin the finish, but will degrade the integrity of the clay, causing it to dissolve.

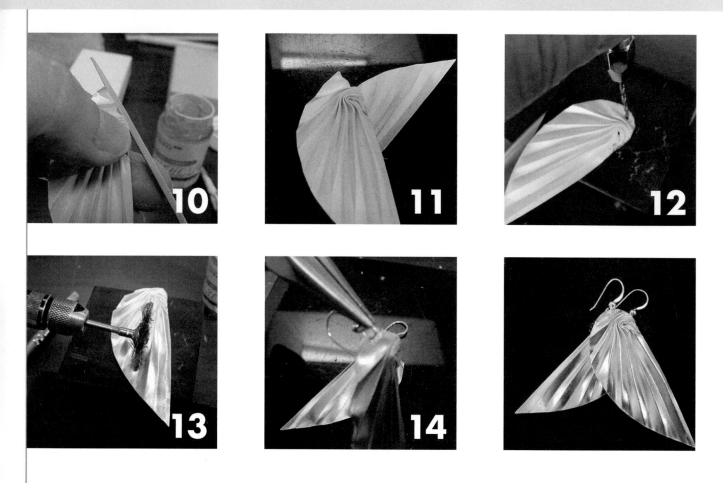

9. Allow to air dry. Excessive heat will cause the Paper Type to crack and fall apart.

10. After completely dry, take a fine file and smooth the edges.

11. Set the pieces on fiber blanket and fire in a cold kiln to 1472°F for 30 minutes. Allow to cool naturally.

12. Lock the drill bit in the pin vise and carefully drill a hole at the top of the round curve, about $^1/_8$" from the edge.

13. With the stainless steel brush loaded in the mini power tool (Dremel, Sears Craftsman or similar), gently remove the white coating. Continue polishing until a bright satin finish is achieved.

14. Attach the French wires so that the earrings hang freely.

15. A variation would be to draw designs on the finished earrings with nail polish and then dip in Liver of Sulfur. Remove the nail polish with nail polish remover and use a soft cloth to polish.

Enjoy!

Basic Project
Caped Glass Pendant

Arlene Hildebrand

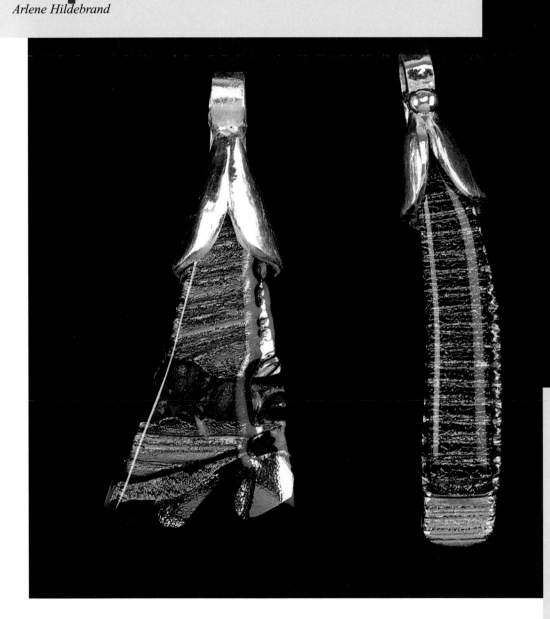

MATERIALS
- 10 grams 650 Lowfire Art Clay
- 2 grams 650 Lowfire Paste Type
- 1-3 grams 650 Lowfire Syringe Type
- Glass cabochon–choose a triangular shape or a long, narrow shape
- Plastic straw
- Roller
- 1mm thickness guides, 2
- 4"x 4" Teflon sheet
- Dental tool with scooped bottom (spatula style)
- Straight edge blade
- Craft knife
- Parchment paper or circle template
- Hairdryer or food dehydrator
- Kiln
- Wire brush

This is listed as a basic Art Clay project, though the use of colorful dichroic glass raises the result a cut above the usual. And it is the use of 650 Lowfire clay that makes it all possible without an expert's knowledge of glass, annealing, or compatibility.

Making the Cape

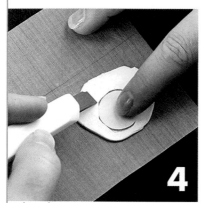

Making the Cape

Making the Cape

Instructions

Making the Cape

1. Decide placement of silver cape on glass cabochon. Measure the width of the cabochon at the widest point of coverage (this will be the bottom of the cape when it is positioned on the cabochon). This measured width should not be more than $^{3}/_{4}$".

2. Using parchment paper draw a circle or use a circle template of the following diameter:

   If the measure in Step 1 is less than $^{1}/_{2}$", your circle diameter should be one inch.

   If the measure in Step 1 is $^{1}/_{2}$" or more your circle diameter should be $1^{1}/_{2}$".

3. Gently knead 10gms of 650 clay and form into a pancake. Place clay pancake on Teflon sheet. Using 1mm thickness guides roll out clay maintaining circular layout. This can be done by rolling clay in different directions, simply remember to keep roller on the thickness guides.

4. Lay parchment paper circle or circle template on clay and using craft knife blade cut out your clay circle.

5. Place your glass cabochon on the clay circle in the upper central half of the circle.

6. Using the spatula lift up the sides of the clay circle and securely drape the clay around the glass cabochon. The seam of the clay cape should be closed, use paste if needed to secure the closure. The closure can extend the length of the cape or at a minimum, from the top of the cape to three-quarters of the length of the cape. The key here is to secure the glass cabochon within the cape. Doing so will ensure that the fired silver cape will securely hold the glass cabochon.

7. Leaving the glass cabochon inside the cape, completely dry the piece. Drying can be accomplished with a hairdryer or by placing the piece in a food dehydrator.

8. After piece is dry, file and sand to smooth rough edges.

9. If desired decorate cape using syringe, dry completely.

10. Set piece aside and make the bail.

Making the Cape

Making the Cape

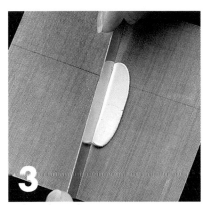

Making the Bail

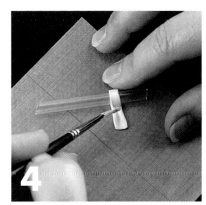

Making the Bail

Making the Bail

1. Using 3 grams of 650 Lowfire clay, gently knead and form into an oblong shape.

2. Lay clay on Teflon sheet and using thickness guides roll out clay maintaining elongated shape.

3. Using a straight edge blade trim and straighten all sides of clay.

4. Place piece of plastic straw at top of long clay strip and using a spatula, lift the top of the clay and guide it up and over the straw. Take clay completely over and around the straw one complete turn. Secure this round clay bail top onto the clay stem with Paste Type. Trim the remaining stem of the bail as desired.

5. Dry piece

6. Trim and sand as needed.

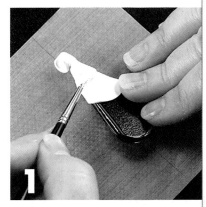

Finishing

Finishing the Piece

1. Using 650 Paste, secure the back of the cape to the stem of the bail.

2. Dry completely.

3. Check that the bail is securely attached to the piece.

4. Do touch up work as necessary.

5. Fire piece using the following schedule:
    Ramp kiln to 1250°F, taking one hour to do so.
    Hold at 1250°F for 30 minutes. Allow kiln to cool completely before opening.

6. Clean white residue from finished piece using wire brush.

7. Piece may be polished using a tumbler.

Finishing

Finishing

Glass-topped Ring

Julie Rorden

MATERIALS

- 10 grams of Art Clay Silver Clay Type
- Bullseye fused dichroic glass cab approximately $^3/_8$" x $^5/_8$", use a dark or opaque base
- Glass cleaner
- Nonporous work surface that is smooth, flat, and hard
- Nonstick baking sheet
- Acrylic roller with $^1/_8$" diameter O-rings on each end; using a thicker O-ring produces a thicker ring shank
- Ring sizer
- Ruler
- Tissue-slicing blade
- Craft knife
- Set of small metal files or optional electric rotary tools
- Non-tapered (step) ring mandrel
- Toaster oven, dehydrator, or hairdryer
- Small cube of non-drying modeling clay
- 1 wedged shaped cosmetic sponge
- Small programmable kiln
- Fiber paper
- Fiber blanket
- 1" kiln posts, 2
- 3" kiln post with rounded corners
- Tongs
- Small metal container with water for quenching
- Small stainless steel brush
- Agate burnisher or smooth metal burnisher
- Wet/dry sand paper, 600, 1200, 2000 grit
- Metal polish
- Soft cloth
- Epoxy (Optional)

The slumped glass ring project is a direct result of one of my many "what-if" moments that tend to occur just after cleaning up my workbench for the day. Several hours and a messy bench later, I pulled a ring out of the kiln unlike any I'd ever done before.

When showing off my curious piece of workmanship, the responses started to become predictable. First comes the touch test. Customers and artist friends will gently glide their fingers over the glass and silver feeling how smooth, cool, and solid to the touch the ring is. Next comes the light test. Not only are they fascinated with the way the reflecting light on the dichroic glass and silver seems to play tricks on their eyes, but they try to figure out how the glass is held in place. Then comes the strength test. Even though these rings are not unbreakable, mine have withstood being poked, pulled, squeezed, frozen, tumbled, stepped on, and dropped on carpeted floors. And finally, the size test: This is my favorite test, the one where they find the right size finger for the ring, slide it on and stroll out the door with a smile on their face because they know they have a one-of-a-kind piece of wearable art on their hand.

The following project is simply a glass cab fused to a cut ring shank. Although the actual physical work time is about an hour or less, the whole process takes several hours because of drying, firing, and annealing times. As you become familiar with this technique and the use of Art Clay, I hope you, too, will experience a lot of enjoyable and surprising "what-if" moments.

Instructions

Slumping Cab

1. Choose a cab that is about half the size of the top of the finger for which you're making the ring. The cab will thin out and stretch a bit as it's slumped over the kiln post.

Slumping Cab

2. Clean fingerprints, dust, and oils from cab with a streak-free glass cleaner.

3. Lay the 3" kiln post on its side, on the center of your raised kiln shelf. Support it with 1" kiln posts on each side so it won't tip over.

4. Cut a 1" x 3" strip of fiber paper and place it on top the rounded corner of the 3" kiln post. Fire to 1200°F. Open the kiln door to cool (the purpose for prefiring the fiber paper is to provide a soft felt-like base for the cab to rest on).

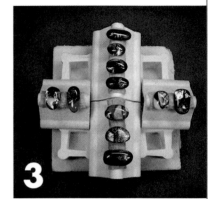

Slumping Cab

5. Balance the cab on the prefired fiber paper. At this point, you may want to slump a number of cabs at once to maximize the use of your time and equipment. The extra slumped cabs can be used for rings, earrings, or necklaces.

6. Fire the cabs at 1550°F for 3minutes (large cabs) to 10 minutes (small cabs) until desired curve is achieved. Curve needs to be about $\frac{1}{8}$" steeper than the curve of your ring so there's room for the glass to move and fuse to your ring shank. No ramping is necessary. Larger cabs require less time to slump because gravity pulls the ends down faster. If fired too long, the cab will thin out and become weak or break in the center. Anneal the cab until room temperature.

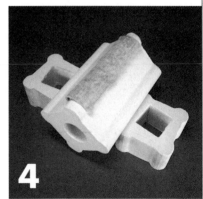

Slumping Cab

Ring Shank

1. While the cab is slumping in the kiln, cut and tape a $\frac{3}{4}$" band of nonstick baking sheet around your ring mandrel. Open and place your clay on another piece of nonstick baking sheet and roll into the shape of a band approximately $\frac{1}{2}$" wide and 3" long. The O-rings on the ends of your roller will provide even depth and the nonstick baking sheet will allow you to easily lift the clay off the rolling surface. Because of the clay shrinkage rate, don't roll or sand your clay band thinner than $\frac{1}{16}$" for this project or the ring strength will be compromised.

2. Using your tissue-slicing blade, cut the clay band to $\frac{3}{8}$" wide and the length needed to go completely around your finger. To allow for clay shrinkage, make the ring band 1 to $1\frac{1}{2}$ sizes larger than you want the finished ring to be. Tightly seal the extra clay for future use.

Slumping Cab

3. Wrap your trimmed clay strip around the mandrel and roughly seal the edges together. Don't worry about making your seam look nice because it'll be cut away later to make room for the cab. Because about 80 percent or more of the finishing work on the ring is done after it's dry—but before firing—don't spend a lot of time fussing with the clay at this point. Completely dry the clay using a toaster oven, dehydrator or hairdryer until it looks almost white. A safe drying temperature is 175°F or less.

4. The dried clay is fragile but, like most greenware, still stable enough to be easily carved and smoothed. Using the modeling clay as support if needed, shape your ring by sanding, filing, or carving. Finally, use a damp cosmetic sponge to smooth the outside and inside of your ring. Remember to round the edges so it'll slide comfortably on and off your finger.

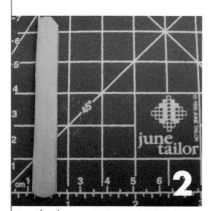

Ring Shank

Ring Shank

5. Place the cab on the ring directly over the seam. Mark and file away the cab area. Save the clay filings, mix with a few drops of water, and use in the future as slip for another project.

6. Next to firing the silver and annealing the glass at the correct temperatures, this is the most critical step of all. Because only a very thin layer of glass fuses to the silver, the edges of the ring shank where the cab will rest need to be gouged out and roughed up with your craft knife or electric rotary tool. Creating a rough surface gives the glass a better surface on which to adhere.

7. Lay the ring on a thin layer of refractory fiber for support and fire at 1600°F for 10 minutes. Open the kiln door and cool to approximately 900°F. Pick the ring up with your tongs and quench in cool water.

Fusing

1. Cut another strip of fiber paper ⅝" wide and long enough to roll into a tube that fits entirely inside the ring. Tightly pack the paper tube with pre-fired (for denser pack) refractory fiber. Place the packed ring on a nest of refractory fiber on the kiln shelf with the cut out area facing up. Make sure the ring is absolutely vertical so the glass doesn't slip off before fusing to the silver.

2. Place the cleaned cab on the cut out area and fire again at 1550°F for 3 minutes (large cabs) to 10 minutes (small cabs). Anneal ring in the kiln until room temperature.

Finishing

1. To remove the white oxidized coating on the fired silver, brush the entire piece with a small stainless steel brush.

2. If you want more luster on the silver, use firm, even strokes with an agate burnisher. Pressing too hard in any one area will dent or scratch the surface. For a mirror finish, use wet/dry 600-, 1200- and 2000-grit sandpaper respectively.

3. Polish the ring using metal polish on a soft cloth.

4. (Optional) If you think the ring is going to get a lot of rough use, consider putting a drop of epoxy at the top and bottom of each end of the cab where it's fused to the silver.

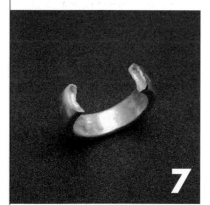

Ring Shank

Fusing

Finishing

Remember that this is just a departure point. Your rings—or other jewelry—should be a product of your own creative explorations with Art Clay Silver!

A Clay by Any Other Name is Porcelain

Basic Project

Windy City Pendant

Judi Hendricks and Jackie Truty

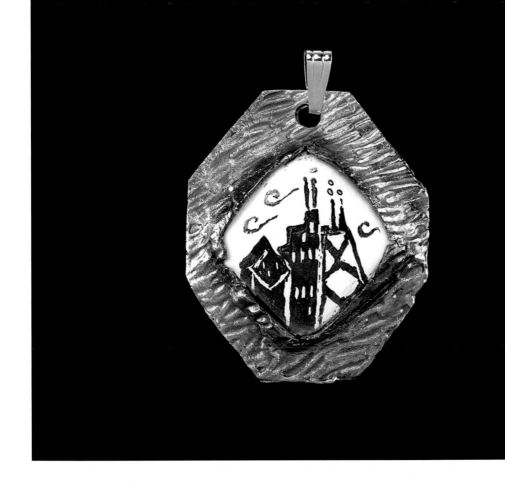

MATERIALS
- 20 gms 650 Lowfire clay
- 15gms 650 Silver Overlay Paste
- Small amount 650 Paste Type
- Plastic re-sealable bag
- Glazed porcelain cabochon, 1" x 1"
- Straw
- Snap-on bail
- Scissors
- Carbon paper
- Tracing paper
- Pencil
- Paintbrush
- Craft knife
- 6" flex blade
- Non-stick work surface
- Roller
- Texture plates
- Dry Liver of Sulfur
- Sgraffito pen or pointed wooden dowel
- Olive oil
- Denatured alcohol
- Cotton swab
- 600 grit sandpaper
- Fine files
- Agate burnisher
- Stainless steel brush
- Straw

Though this project uses a porcelain cabochon, similar projects can be made using any porcelain or glass shapes, including picture frames, spoons, even shards of broken china.

Windy City design

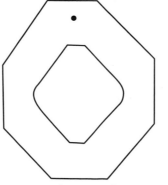

Windy City template

Instructions

1. Wet a cotton swab with denatured alcohol and squeeze out excess. Carefully wipe both sides of the porcelain cab to remove traces of clay, oil and dirt. Allow to dry.

2. In a small, shallow container, dilute a small amount of Silver Overlay Paste with a few drops of water until the consistency of skim milk. It is important that the Overlay Paste be thin enough to "float" on the surface of the porcelain. If the paste is too thick, it will chip off when you try to scratch the design into it.

3. Using a clean paintbrush, apply a very thin layer of the dilute Overlay Paste onto the surface of the porcelain cab. It should be thin enough to be nearly translucent. Dry well.

4. Cut a small piece of the carbon paper to fit onto the cab and cover with your chosen design (a suggestion appears on page 99). With a pencil or toothpick, trace the design very lightly. When you remove the design and the carbon paper, the design should be visible on the dried layer of Overlay Paste. Remember you are essentially creating a reverse stencil or negative image.

5. Take the sgraffito pen or sharpened wooden dowel (or chopstick!) and trace the design, removing all excess Overlay Paste and leaving the design. Brush very gently to clean the surface. Any Overlay Paste dust that remains on the porcelain will be fired on permanently.

6. Turn the pendant over gently and with the paintbrush decorate the reverse of the porcelain cab with Silver Overlay Paste. Dry.

7. Trace outline of template (page 99) onto tracing paper and cut out. Lay aside.

8. Open 20 grams of Art Clay 650 Lowfire Clay, cut in half and put half away in plastic bag until later.

9. Roll 10 grams of clay into ball and roll out into general shape of template on non-stick surface. Transfer to oiled texture plate and roll out to slightly larger than template.

10. Take 6" flex blade and cut excess exterior clay away. Then switch to craft knife and cut out center according to template.

11. Take straw and punch a hole $\frac{1}{16}$" from center top.

12. Carefully peel clay from texture plate and place back on non-stick surface. Dry thoroughly.

13. When dry, flip over so textured side is down, and wet edge of center hole with a damp paintbrush. Center porcelain cab over hole.

14. Remove second, 10gm of clay from bag and repeat Steps 3 through 5.

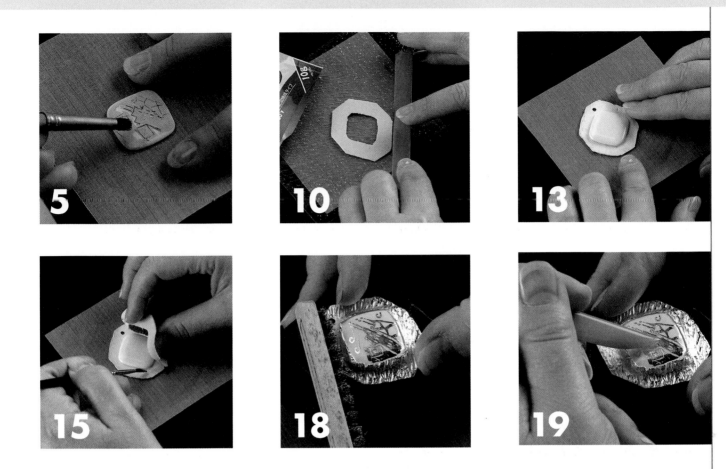

15. Paint a thin layer of Paste Type on bottom layer around porcelain cab and peel off top layer of clay from texture plate, placing it over the bottom layer, sandwiching the cab between the two layers of clay. Press the edges gently and fill any gaps on the edges with Paste Type. Dry.

16. Using fine files and 600 grit sandpaper, even the edges and border of clay around cabochon. Use a round file to clean the hole.

17. Place the pendant on a fiberboard and fire in a kiln at 1250°F for 30 minutes. Let cool naturally.

18. Remove finished pendant from kiln and use stainless steel brush on both sides of silver clay border ONLY. Do NOT use brush on porcelain cabochon.

19. Use the agate burnisher on the sgraffito design, bringing it to a high shine.

20. Mix Liver of Sulfur as indicated on page 39. String a scrap piece of wire through the hole in the top of the pendant and dip the entire pendant into the hot Liver of Sulfur until black. Remove, rinse in clear water and dry.

21. Brush the outside clay portion with the stainless steel brush until only the recessed portions remain black.

22. Buff the entire piece with a soft cloth. Do NOT use silver polish or you will remove the black patina. Attach snap on pendant bail and add chain to finish.

Note: For a change of pace, dip piece only briefly to create a fall color palette.

Basic Project

Cork Clay Heart Pendant

Maria Martinez

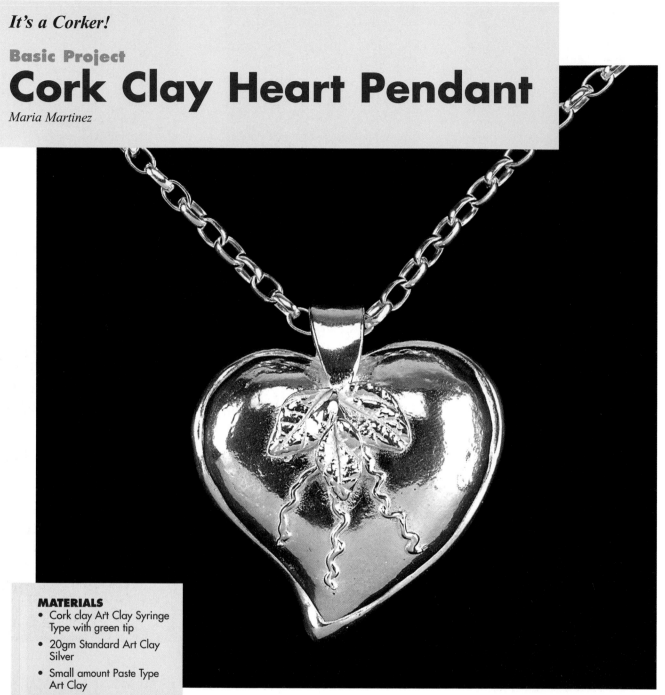

MATERIALS

- Cork clay Art Clay Syringe Type with green tip
- 20gm Standard Art Clay Silver
- Small amount Paste Type Art Clay
- Plastic slats
- Craft knife
- 600 and 1200 grit sandpaper
- Teflon coated sheet
- Paintbrush
- Roller
- Olive oil
- Wire brush
- Straw

And you thought the only other uses for cork (aside from wine bottle stoppers) were to make coasters and compasses! Cork clay is ground cork with a water-soluble binder that is used as a form on which to build a shell of silver in whatever shape you desire. Because it burns to ash in the kiln, it is far superior to paper clay, which does not, and far safer than plastic foam, which gives off toxic fumes as it burns.

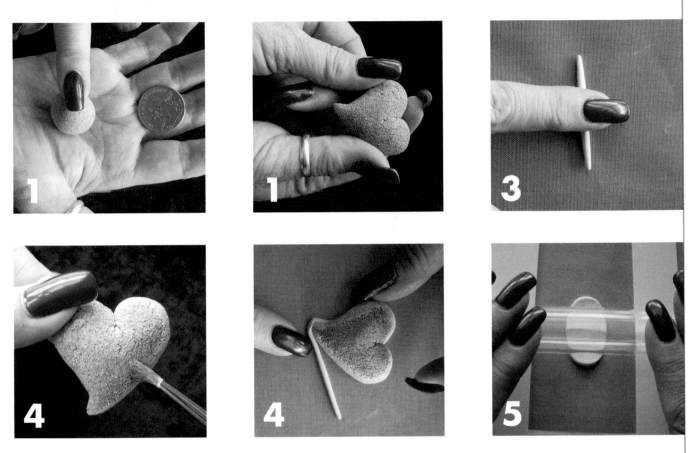

Instructions

1. Using your fingers, shape a small amount of cork clay into a ball approximately the size of a quarter. Shape into a heart creating a bit of a dome. Set aside to dry. The cork clay must be completely dry before continuing with the project. (I usually let dry overnight.)

2. From the 20 gm of Art Clay Silver, pinch off about a third for the first coil. Wrap the rest of the clay in a plastic bag to prevent it from drying.

3. Apply a bit of olive oil to the Teflon sheet. This will be your work surface. Roll out the clay into a long coil, as even as possible, about the diameter of a strand of spaghetti. Make it long enough to go around the entire outer edge of the heart.

4. Add a bit of paste all around the edges of the heart. Also add paste to the coil so it will adhere to the heart better. Where the coil meets, cut off any excess with a craft knife. Add paste with a small brush to both ends and press together. Smooth with paintbrush. Let dry.

5. On the Teflon sheet, roll out the rest of the Art Clay Silver between the two plastic slats. The thickness should not exceed 1mm. Keep turning the clay to maintain a round shape.

6. Cover the entire heart with the rolled out clay. With your fingers, gently press the clay to the shape of the heart.

7. Using a craft knife trim the excess clay from around the heart. Trim along side the coil. Save all excess Art Clay Silver to be used later for a bail, coil #2, and for leaves. Wrap the clay in a plastic bag to prevent it from drying.

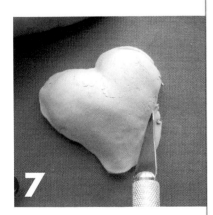

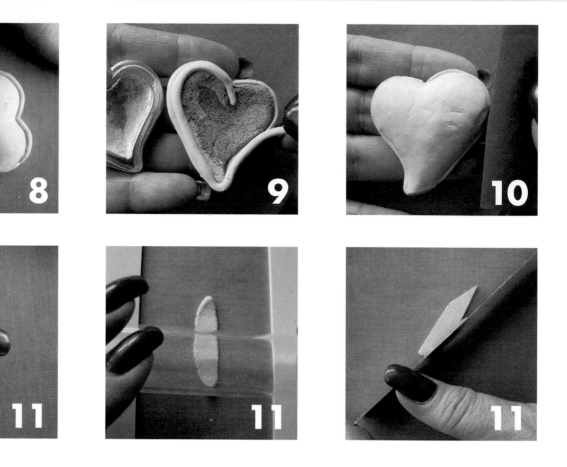

8. Using the small paintbrush, add Paste Type to seal the joint between the clay and the coil. Let dry.

9. For visual and structural support, roll out a thin coil from the excess Art Clay Silver long enough to go around the inside edge of the reverse side of the heart. Add paste to coil #2 and attach to the inside edge of coil #1. Add additional paste as needed to seal any gaps. Let dry.

10. Sand the entire heart with 600 grit sandpaper. Repair any deep cracks or pits with Syringe Type and smooth with a damp brush. Let dry and sand again with 600 grit sandpaper. When smooth, sand with 1200 grit sandpaper. Brush loose silver powder from the piece.

11. For the bail, take a large pea-sized piece of Art Clay Silver and roll slightly. Flatten the clay with a roller to about 1mm thick. Make sure it will be long enough to go around the straw and also connect to the main pendant. Using a craft knife cut the desired shape and length.

12. Fold the clay over the straw, forming the bail.

13. Add paste to the bail where it attaches to the pendant and press into place, aligning properly. Add more paste if needed to seal the joint. Dry thoroughly.

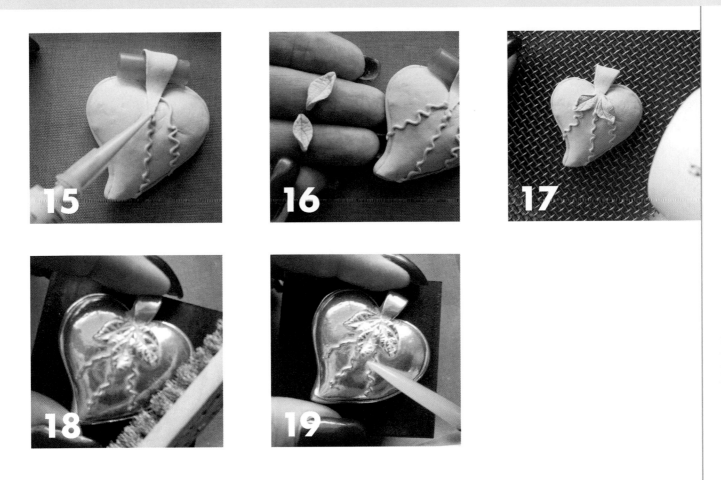

14. Sand any rough edges on the bail with 600 and 1200 grit sandpapers

15. Extrude a design of squiggly lines using an Art Clay Syringe with a green tip. Be sure to keep the syringe, tip down, in a cup of water to prevent the clay from drying in the tip.

16. To make the leaves, take a pea-sized piece of clay and shape it into a leaf. Press it into a mold of a leaf or freeform. Add details, such as veins, and dry. Add paste to the back of the leaf and on the heart where they will join. Press the leaf to the heart.

17. Use a hairdryer or dehydrator to dry your piece thoroughly. Place your completed heart pendant on a fiber blanket upside down, so the cork clay is on top. Fire at 1472°F for 30 minutes.

18. Use a wire brush to reveal a satin finish.

19. Use a burnisher on the raised areas, or place in a rotary tumbler with stainless steel shot, water and jewelry cleaner for at least 1½ hours until shiny. This also helps to work-harden the piece.

20. The piece is complete. Add a chain to finish.

Inro Lidded Pendant

Design by Patricia Walton
Pendant by Jackie Truty

MATERIALS

- 20gms Art Clay, Clay Type
- Paste Type (used to connect piece and fill any gaps)
- Syringe Type with the blue and green tips (used to decorate)
- Cork clay
- 28" round black rubber or leather cord or snake chain
- Bailbacks, 4
- Roller
- 1mm cardboard strips or boards, 2
- Craft knife
- Tissue blade
- Teflon sheet
- Nonstick work surface
- Fiber paper
- Paintbrushes, flat and round
- Water container
- Cosmetic sponge
- Plastic wrap
- Wet/Dry sandpaper, 600, 1200 grit
- Round nose pliers
- Small plastic box
- Tweezers
- Wire brush
- Rubber block
- Burnisher
- SC2 Paragon Programmable Kiln
- Firing board
- Fiber cloth
- Tongs
- Fine steel wool

The pendant is a hollow container created using Clay Type, Paste Type, and Syringe Type over a form made of cork clay. It is not a project for the faint of heart, but perseverance and attention to detail will result in an heirloom piece.

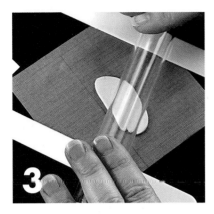  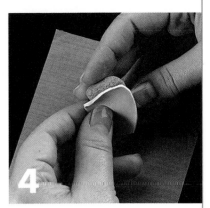

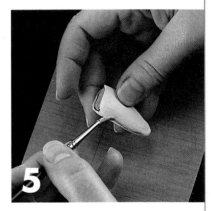

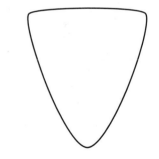

Instructions

1. Begin the project by shaping a ¾" ball of cork clay into the desired bullet shape. Use the drawing to create the cork shape. The top is an oval shape and the edges taper to a knife point. Flatten the top by pressing onto your work surface. Dry overnight or place in a dehydrator. The cork clay must be completely dry before adding the Art Clay. Any moisture in the cork will create steam and cause problems during firing.

2. Once dry, file, and sand the cork form smooth. The finished piece will reflect the cork form. If the cork is rough and uneven, the finished piece will be also. Place the cork form onto a piece of paper and draw around to create a pattern. Add one millimeter to the measurement around the cork form to compensate for the thickness of the Art Clay.

3. Open 20 grams of Art Clay, Clay Type onto a Teflon sheet. Place the 1mm cardboard strips or boards on each side of the Art Clay and roll out using the roller supported on the 1mm boards. If you have trouble with the Art Clay drying out cover the Art Clay and the 1mm cardboard or wooden strips with plastic wrap before rolling out. Next remove the strips and continue to roll a very small amount more. Use the paper pattern to determine the size needed. Cut out two shapes using the pattern. Wrap any left over pieces tightly in plastic wrap or airtight container for later use.

4. Moisten each clay piece with a damp brush and place one on each side of the cork form with the upper edges of the clay pieces just below the top edge of the cork form. Where the two layers meet, lay down a line of Syringe Type using the blue or green tip onto the cork form. Press the edges together and smooth with a flat damp brush. Dry.

5. When dry, file edges and fill any needed areas.

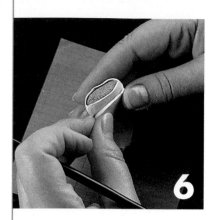

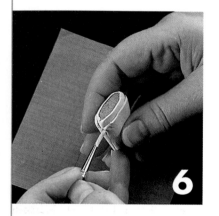

6. Measure ¼" from the top of the pattern and trim off. Using this new pattern, cut out two more clay shapes. Dampen pieces as in Step 2. Lightly moisten the dried clay before placing the two new pieces over the first, lining up the tops ¼" below the first layer and easing the seams together. This will create the lip for the lid. Dampen edges and press together then dry.

7. Reshape each bailback into a horseshoe by using a pair of round nose pliers. Attach one bailback on either side, lining up the tabs with the lip of the second layer of clay. Cover tabs completely with Paste or Syringe Type. Completely dry the piece before continuing.

8. Producing a perfect 1mm coil: A smooth plastic box and a nonstick work surface are the perfect tools to roll out a coil of Art Clay. Form a coil about the diameter of a soda straw by hand. Place the coil on a nonstick work surface, gently pass the smooth plastic box or piece of glass quickly back and forth over the coil until the 1mm coil is created. You can check to see if the coil is the proper thickness by placing the 1mm cardboard strips on each side of the coil and then placing the plastic box or glass on top. Brush the coil with water to prevent cracking. Dampen the outside, lower edge of the piece. Then brush on a layer of Paste Type and attach the 1mm coil to the outside edge of the second layer, around the bailbacks. Trim to fit, pasting the seam. Fill any spaces around the bailbacks with Paste Type, being careful to keep the holes open.

9. Once dry, fill, file, and sand the piece with 600 and 1200 grit sandpapers so there are no visible cracks.

10. Cut a piece of fiber paper ¼" wide and long enough to fit perfectly around the outside lip of the piece. This is the area that was not covered by the second layer of Art Clay. The ends should not overlap. Dampen slightly to get the fiber paper to adhere to the piece.

11. Roll out a piece of Art Clay 1 mm thick, ¼" wide and long enough to wrap around the dried piece of the fiber paper. Close seam and dry the piece.

12. File the upper edge level before creating the top of the lid. Roll out Art Clay 1mm thick and an oval large enough to cover the top of the piece. Dampen the edge of the lid side with water and then add a small amount of Paste Type. Place the piece upside down onto the rolled out clay and trim to fit with a craft knife. Dry, fill, and sand the lid.

13. Shape and apply two more bailbacks as in Step 7. Next, as in Step 7, roll out a coil of Art Clay; this coil is attached to the outside of the upper edge of the lid around the bailbacks. Dry completely.

14. Gently remove the lid. Decide placement of roses and leaves. Remove and discard the fiber paper.

15. Finish the piece using 600 and then 1200 grit sandpaper and finally a makeup sponge. Be sure to check the inside of the lid to make sure it still easily fits the bottom part. This is the most critical stage of the project. Both the bottom of the vessel and the lid should appear as if they are one piece of clay, with no seams, pits, holes, or bumps visible.

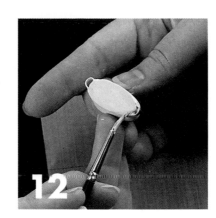

16. This example is decorated with roses and leaves, but stones, Paper Type cutouts, syringe work, or other sculpted flowers and leaves can be used. For stones, see the section on stone setting on page 22.

17. For easy flowers, cut long, thin, narrow triangles of Art Clay. Dampen top slightly and roll from point to wide end. Repeat in several different sizes. Create leaves from rice- to pear-sized pieces of Art Clay, shaping and using a toothpick to form veins. Dry.

18. Using Syringe Type with blue and green tips, create a lattice pattern on the front of the vessel and the top of the lid. Then, using a small amount of Paste Type, place leaves and flowers in an aesthetically pleasing design. Dry. Fill any gaps with Paste Type. Sand very lightly. Finish the pre-polishing by wiping with a barely damp cosmetic sponge.

19. Using fiber blanket as support, place the lid right side up on a fiber board. Prop the body up so that the cork clay opening is facing up. Fire in a kiln at 1472°F for 30 minutes. The cork will cause smoke. Do not open the kiln door after beginning the firing, as the added oxygen will result in open flame.

20. To clean and polish, support pieces on a rubber block. Use a wire brush for a matt finish and then use a burnisher on the edges, bezels, and decorations to create a high polish. The inside may be cleaned with fine steel wool. If the lid does not fit properly, file or sand the lip area. Run a cord or chain through the bailback holes. Knot the ends of the cord or add beads. If using a chain, add jump rings and dangle beads.

Basic/Advanced Project
Art Clay and Old Lace Bezel Brooch

Deb Jemmott

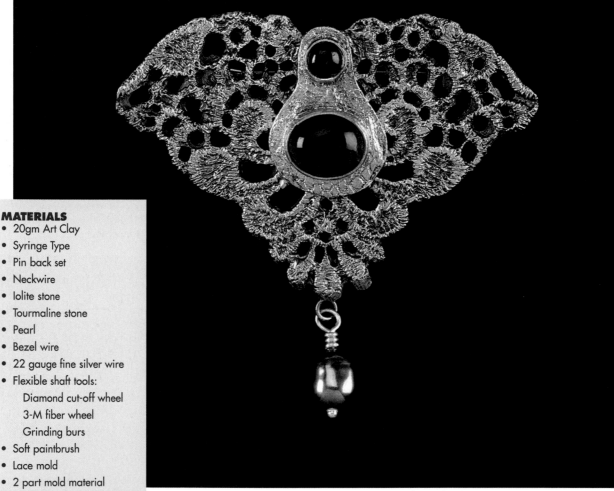

MATERIALS
- 20gm Art Clay
- Syringe Type
- Pin back set
- Neckwire
- Iolite stone
- Tourmaline stone
- Pearl
- Bezel wire
- 22 gauge fine silver wire
- Flexible shaft tools:
    Diamond cut-off wheel
    3-M fiber wheel
    Grinding burs
- Soft paintbrush
- Lace mold
- 2 part mold material
- Jeweler's round nose pliers
- Bezel-setting tools
- Agate burnisher
- Liver of Sulfur
- Stiff brass brush
- Rubber bench block
- Setting tools
- Tongs
- Gloves
- Water
- Epoxy

There are many variations to this piece, beginning with the choice of lace and stones. This article is meant as an inspirational instruction guide more than a "how to" make an exact copy of this piece. I would consider this an advanced level piece, although many of the techniques can be broken out and used independently as beginning or intermediate projects. This piece encompasses many Art Clay techniques as well as traditional jewelry techniques.

Instructions

Making the Mold

Any lace may be used, but thicker, more dimensional lace works best.

1. Attach the lace to a clean, dry, flat surface with double-sided tape. The "right" side should be up.

2. Use a two-part mold material (Art Clay sells one). Mix the mold material well. Pat it out into a flat piece that is approximately the size and shape of the lace. Place it on the lace and press the mold material into the lace. There should be at least 2mm or 3mm of mold material over the lace.

3. Let it cure completely.

4. Pull the mold material up and remove the lace.

Making the Mold

The Pin Back

1. The pin back assembly is made up of four parts: two nuts with threaded holes, a pin stem and a catch. The pin stem and catch have threaded parts that fit into the nuts. The pin stem and the catch should NOT go through the firing process, but the respective nuts will be inserted into the clay and fired in place. Screw the pin stem into one nut; screw the catch into the other nut. Be sure they are screwed in all the way, as this will determine the position of the nuts in the finished piece. The pin stem has a "spring" that, in its resting position, keeps it slightly above the catch. Do not insert it into the catch when the pieces are placed into the wet clay or the nut holding the pin stem will lean over.

2. Prepare the pin back pieces before beginning to work in the clay.

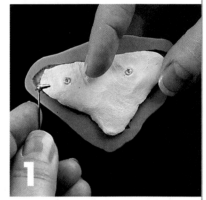

The Pin Back

Back Lace Piece

1. Pack Art Clay into the mold. Keep the thickness as even as possible, but cover the mold entirely. There should be about 1mm of clay over the uppermost parts of the mold. Immediately insert the pin stem nut (with the pin stem in place) into the back of the piece. The pin stem will not be perpendicular to the back of the piece, as the spring will make it stand up a little. Under the tip of the pin stem, insert the catch nut (with the catch in place) into the back of the piece. Keep the nuts perpendicular to the piece.

2. With the pin back assembly in place, leave the lace back piece in the mold to dry. Removing it early risks damaging the image.

3. Once the piece is completely dry, leave the clay in the mold and gently unscrew the pin stem and the catch. Be careful to keep the nuts in position. Use syringe to fill in the area around the nut, but *do not* let clay get into the hole. Use a damp paintbrush to smooth the syringe work into the back of the piece.

4. Starting at the edges of the mold, gently pull the mold away from the clay. Remove the clay. Dry thoroughly before beginning the next step.

5. To set up for carving with a flex shaft, fold a piece of paper in half to use as a work surface to catch the Art Clay dust. This can be reconstituted into clay. Flex shaft tools you will need: Diamond cut-off wheel, 3-M fiber wheel, and grinding burs.

Back Lace Piece

Back Lace Piece

Back Lace Piece

Making the Bezels

Making the Bezels

Making the Bezels

6. Use the diamond cut off wheel to carve the outside edges. Work at a slow to medium speed with a very light touch. Use a soft paintbrush to wipe the Art Clay dust off to see the piece better. Be sure to support the piece well throughout the carving process, as the greenware is very delicate. To carve small areas, use the edge of the wheel. To carve large areas, use the flat of the wheel. This same work can be accomplished by hand with files.

7. Clean up the back of the piece using a 3-M fiber wheel on the flex shaft. Support the piece well. Use a light touch. The piece can be left with the slight marks of the fiber wheel or a finer finish can be achieved by using a baby wipe after the fiber wheel.

8. Use a small, pointed grinding bur to make holes in the piece where there are indentations from the mold. Support the piece well and work with a light touch. Use a soft paintbrush to clean the Art Clay dust off the piece to see what areas should be carved. The same mold can be used to create many different pieces when various sections are carved away.

Making the Bezels

1. Choose an appropriate height bezel for the stone. The bezel should be tall enough to mechanically hold the stone in place while covering as little of it as possible plus 1mm to be buried in the clay.

2. Make sure one end of the bezel wire is flat and straight. Cutting the bezel with flush cutters is sometimes sufficient. If the wire does not have a flat end after cutting, it will need to be filed.

3. Use round nose pliers to gently bend the flat, straight end to fit around the stone. Don't squeeze the bezel wire with the pliers, but instead use the pliers as a mandrel to shape it to match the stone. The end (and ultimately the joint) should be on the "long" side of the stone and never on a point.

4. Place the stone and the partially-fitted bezel on a flat surface and gently wrap the bezel all the way around the stone. Keep the bezel perpendicular to the tabletop—don't let it fold over the stone. Continue working the bezel until it fits the stone well with no large gaps.

5. Mark where the bezel overlaps and cut on the long side of the line. File the end if necessary.

6. The ends of the bezel should meet together perfectly along the entire length of the seam. The stone should easily move in and out of the bezel. To test the bezel, set it on a flat surface and make sure the stone will go in from the top. When it is in place, there should be no large gaps between the stone and the bezel. Reshape the bezel as necessary to fit the stone.

Front Lace Piece

1. Make a paper pattern of the piece to fit under the stones.

2. Roll out the clay a little thicker than usual; about $1\frac{1}{2}$ mm thick.

3. Place a thin, flat lace on the rolled out clay and roll again, imprinting the clay.

4. Pull the lace off.

5. Place the pattern on an interesting area of the design. Cut around the pattern using a craft knife.

6. Remove the extra clay. Place the bezels on the lace front piece and press them evenly into the clay. Press them approximately $\frac{3}{4}$ of the way through the clay, being careful not to go all the way through.

7. Dry completely.

8. Clean up and shape the edges of the front lace piece with a file.

9. Use paste to secure the bezels inside and out. Place the paste only where the bezel joins the clay and where the bezel joins itself. Be careful to not use much paste inside the bezel or it can make the area too small for the stone.

10. Dry completely.

Assembling the Piece

1. Paint Art Clay Paste under the front lace piece and place it on the back lace piece. Use a damp brush to smooth any excess clay. If there are cracks or spaces, use paste or syringe to fill them and a damp brush to smooth the pieces together.

2. Check the back. Use a wet paintbrush to smooth any clay that came through the holes.

3. Clean the top and outside of the bezel wire with a craft knife. Do *not* clean the paste out of the seam area.

4. Using jeweler's round nose pliers, twist a 1" long piece of 22 gauge fine silver wire to make the loop for the pearl. Leave extra wire and bend outward. The extra wire makes the piece easier to attach and makes the attachment much stronger.

5. Use Syringe Type to attach the wire to the back lace piece. Allow to dry. Fill in areas with more syringe and use a damp paintbrush to smooth into the back lace piece.

Firing and Finishing

1. Place into a programmable kiln and fire the Art Clay at 1600°F for 10 minutes.

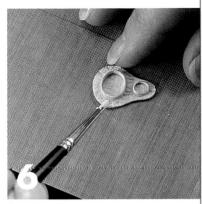

Front Lace Piece

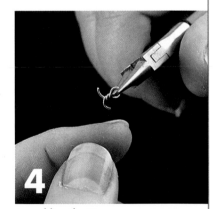

Front Lace Piece

Assembling the Piece

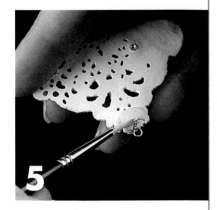

Assembling the Piece

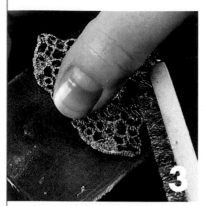

Firing and Finishing

Firing and Finishing

Firing and Finishing

2. Remove, using glove and tongs, and quench in cool water.

3. Burnish with a stiff wire brush.

4. Insert the pin stem and pin catch. Be sure they line up. It may be necessary to use some force to get them back into the proper position, but *do not over-screw them.*

5. Remove the pin stem and catch. Put a dab of epoxy in each hole. Replace the pin stem and catch. Latch the pin stem in place, remove any excess glue, and allow the glue to cure.

6. Oxidize the piece with Liver of Sulfur. Highlight areas with a wire brush.

Setting the Stones
1. File or sand the top edge of the bezel. Make sure that it is just tall enough to hold the stone in place, but not so tall that the bezel will have folds in it when it is pressed against the stone. Clean any excess Art Clay off the bezel. Be careful to not clean out the bezel joint. Finish with fine sandpaper to leave a smooth, even finish on the top of the bezel.

2. Check to make sure the bezel still fits the stone. It may have distorted in the clean-up process.

3. Setting the stone is the LAST thing to be done on a piece. All other work on the piece should be done prior to setting the stone. Generally, after the stone is set, re-firing the piece is not possible and clean up is more difficult.

4. Work on a rubber block to prevent the piece from slipping or damaging the back. Use a bezel pusher or a rocker bezel pusher to push the bezel at opposite points in at least eight places before finally setting. The pressure points are opposite in sequence to keep the stone centered. Work around the stone with the bezel pusher until the bezel is against the stone all the way around. Burnish the sides and top of the bezel with an agate burnisher until they are smooth and shiny.

5. Use 22 gauge fine silver wire through the pearl. Loop through the loop on the bottom of the piece and wrap in place.

Basic Project

Capturing the Golden Rose

Judi Hendricks

MATERIALS
- 10-15 grams Art Clay Silver (depending on your design)
- 5 gms Art Clay Gold
- Small amount Art Clay Paste-Type
- Smallest Syringe Type with green tip,
- One 3mm clear CZ
- Teflex non-stick work surface
- Rose or flower mold of your choice
- Cotton swab
- Olive oil
- Wire brush

One of the things I most enjoy about working with and wearing precious metals is the weight of them—the sense of substance. I recall the first time I was given a silver dollar as a child, and thinking what a marvelous tactile thrill it was just to hold it, or to toss it from palm to palm. It was such a seductive sensation that I couldn't bring myself to spend it—and that was back in the days when a whole dollar would have kept us neighborhood kids in candy for a couple of weeks. One of the first things I made when I discovered Art Clay silver was a solid silver acorn, cast from an actual acorn mold, and invariably the reaction people have when I drop it in their hand is to say, "Ooo-ooo! It's heavy!" and then they play with it for five or ten minutes before they can bring themselves to put it down.

This project has several steps and two firings, but it's actually pretty easy, and results in a chunky little pendant that has a lovely heft for its size. I've used a "peg" design to create a decadent, solid gold rose that can be captured into the silver pendant. I love the rich look of the gold against the whiteness of the silver. This design also has metaphysical significance for me, as the golden rose is a symbol of protection and release of negativity.

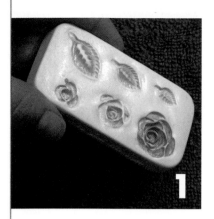

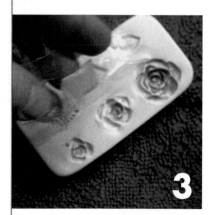

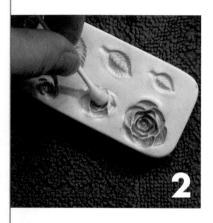

Instructions

1. I found this mold in the polymer clay section of my favorite craft store. It creates some deep, defined roses and has several different-sized rose leaves, which is nice. The one thing I don't like about it is that it's rigid; it can sometimes be a challenge to remove the clay from the mold. Five grams of gold clay will fill the mid-sized rose and leave more than enough back clay to form the "peg."

2. Whenever you work with a mold (but especially if it's a deep female mold like this one) it's a good idea to lubricate the inner surface. I've used silicone and all sorts of fancy release sprays, and frankly, they don't seem to work any better than a simple dab of olive oil, so (being frugal) I use that. Apply sparingly with a cotton swab and then go back and wipe the mold out with the dry end of the swab. You don't want to trap a bubble of oil between the clay and the surface of the mold! Choose your leaf size and oil that as well.

3. Press the gold clay firmly into the mold. When the clay is embedded, pinch up the back of the clay to form a "peg." You want the peg to be irregular in shape and slightly wider at the top than at the base, so that the silver of the pendant will grasp it firmly as it sinters. (You may want to reserve a tiny bit of the gold clay to mix with a drop or two of water and use as paste for repairs to the rose once it's unmolded.)

4. To prevent distortion, I usually leave the clay in the mold until it's completely dry. And I've noticed that when I use my dehydrator to dry clay in a mold, it usually unmolds more easily if I allow it to come to room temperature (or slightly cooler) before removing the rose. This one took a bit of wiggling to remove, but it popped out whole. Check to make sure the face of the rose is dry, and file or sand any burrs. Make sure you retain your gold dust and add it to your gold paste. Fill in any cracks in the rose and dry thoroughly.

5. Once the rose has dried, feel free to etch any details you choose into the front or back surface. One of my metaphysical Art Clay students etched the word "Joy" on the back of her rose. No one was able to see it once it was in place, but she said, "I know it's there, and every time I look at the pendant I remember to be joyful." It's one of the fun pluses of making your own jewelry.

6. Once it's dried and finished, fire the rose. Since gold needs to be fired at a much higher temperature than silver (1814°F for 60 minutes.), it can even be fired days in advance. Once fired, you can buff the rose lightly with a wire brush if you like (I do, just because I love the way it looks), but you don't need to polish it at this point, since it will be undergoing a second firing. And remember that this is 22k gold and fairly soft; be careful not to over-polish and destroy fine detail.

7. The leaves are made out of Art Clay Silver, and are actually quite easy to mold. Since they're not very deep, they can be lifted out of the mold while the clay is still moist. This is the perfect time to add or deepen the veining on the leaves with a craft knife or pin tool, or etch cuts into the sides. These will dry fairly quickly.

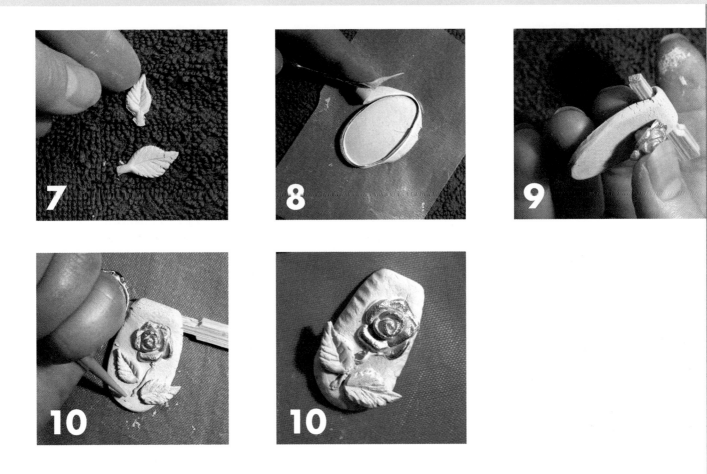

8. I chose a simple oval base with a rollover bail—meaning that the top of the clay is just "rolled over" a wooden cocktail fork and glued to itself. I rolled 10 grams of Art Clay silver out to a 3mm thickness and shaped a bit of bezel-foil into an impromptu cookie-cutter. I didn't intend for the oval to be perfect (I could have hand-cut it with a craft knife); I was just looking for the general shape.

9. Turning the rose over, I painted a generous dab of Art Clay Paste Type onto the ridges of the "peg" prior to inserting it into the pendant. I then pressed the sides of the oval inward (toward the rose, which is slightly offset) to secure the capture, and painted a bit of paste on the back to secure the bail. I pressed the pendant firmly to my Teflex non-stick work surface and continued work on the face.

10. I used paste to glue the leaves to the surface of the pendant, then used syringe clay to pipe in the stem. If you like, you can also capture a 3mm CZ on one side of the stem, table-side **down**, to create a sparkling "thorn." I then let the piece dry, and etched some ragged ridges into the sides with a microfile to add a sort of rugged contrast to the beauty of the gold rose.

11. Since this piece is on the hefty side, it's important to make sure that it's thoroughly dry before putting it in the kiln to fire. If I'm ever in doubt as to whether a piece is fully dry, I err on the side of caution and stick it back in the dehydrator. (I was so loathe to risk damaging this piece that I actually left it in the dehydrator overnight before finishing it.) General guidelines for telling whether a piece is dry are that it's hard—firm to the touch—with no soft spots. Also, moist clay tends to feel cool; dry clay doesn't. And you can always try the vapor test: Place the piece on a stainless steel or dark glass sheet, and after 10~20 seconds pick up the piece. If there is no cloud of water vapor, it's probably dry.

12. Finish the back of the piece as your fancy takes you (you can buff it down to a mirror finish or echo the etched look from the front, for example). Keep in mind that if you want to, you can sand the back down far enough to expose the golden "peg" and use it as a design element. One student of mine sanded down the back of her pendant and used the tiny gold circle as the iris of an etched Egyptian "eye"; another creative lass syringed silver clay around the peg to suggest the rays of a minute golden "sun."

13. Once the pendant is dry and finished to your taste, fire the pendant a second time to sinter the Art Clay silver and capture the golden rose (1472°F for 30 minutes, or 1600°F for 10 minutes). As with all fired pieces, you can now use your wire brush to brush away the powdery "bloom" from the surface of the pendant. If you like the brushed finish, you're done—but you can also go through the steps of wet sanding or put it into a tumbler with stainless-steel shot and tumbling solution and let it polish for a couple of hours.

14. And there you are. A precious protective amulet—a golden rose that will never fade.

Lotsa Heart Solid and Foiled Gold Pendant

Jane Levy

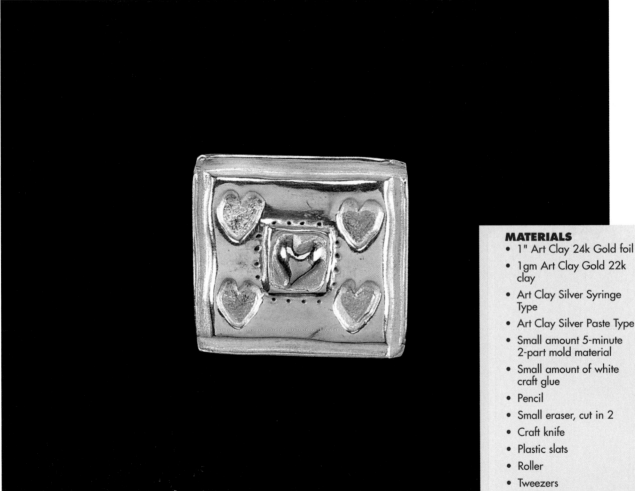

This wonderfully (and deceptively) simple design combines the two most traditional Art Clay gold applications: solid gold (22k) and gold foil (24k).

MATERIALS

- 1" Art Clay 24k Gold foil
- 1gm Art Clay Gold 22k clay
- Art Clay Silver Syringe Type
- Art Clay Silver Paste Type
- Small amount 5-minute 2-part mold material
- Small amount of white craft glue
- Pencil
- Small eraser, cut in 2
- Craft knife
- Plastic slats
- Roller
- Tweezers
- K-008 bailback
- Agate burnisher
- Olive oil
- Large pea size ball of polymer clay
- Small heart paper punch
- Texture plate
- 600, 1200, and 2000 grit sandpapers
- Fiber blanket
- Wenol polish and cloth
- Timer or watch with a second hand

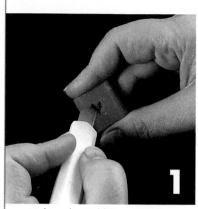

Making the Gold Heart Mold

Making the Gold Heart Mold

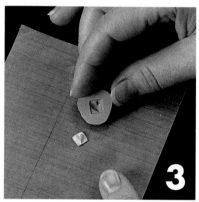

Making the Gold Heart Mold

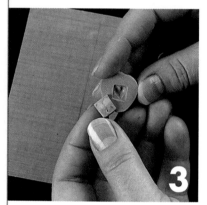

Making the Gold Heart Mold

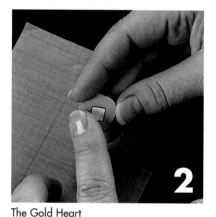

The Gold Heart

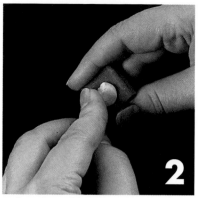

The Gold Heart

Instructions

I. Making the Gold Heart Mold

1. Draw a small heart on an eraser. With a craft knife, cut out around the outline to a depth of approximately 2mm and remove the piece.

2. Take a small amount of polymer clay and press into the eraser mold, creating an even base around the heart. Remove gently and place on a flat surface. With the craft knife, cut excess clay away to leave a small, square base surrounding the heart. Bake according to manufacturer's directions.

3. Mix a small amount of equal parts of 5-minute 2-part mold material until even in color. Flatten slightly. Carefully press cooled, baked polymer clay heart into the mold material until slightly below the surface. Let set until a fingernail pressed into the heart leaves no impression. Remove heart and set aside. Your mold is now ready for use.

II. The Gold Heart

1. Cut one gram of Art Clay gold 22k clay from a 5gm pack (seal remainder in plastic wrap with moist sponge and store for future use). Roll into a small ball. Make sure there are no air bubbles or creases in the clay.

2. Press the gold clay into the previously-created heart mold, filling all areas. Even the top.

3. Allow the gold clay to set about five minutes and then carefully ease the gold heart from the mold by bending the flexible, silicon mold edges away from the clay.

Silver Base

Silver Base

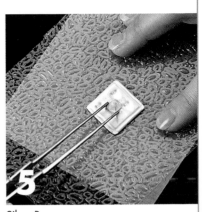

Silver Base

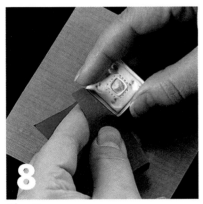

Silver Base

Silver Base

4. Set the gold heart on a flat surface and straighten the edges with a plastic slat or craft knife. Dry thoroughly.

5. Fire the gold clay in a kiln at 1814°F for 1 hour. Cool.

III. Silver Base

1. Carve a small heart stamp (approximately. 3/8") out of the other piece of eraser. Make sure sides are smooth and even.

2. Rub a small amount of olive oil onto one side of a texture plate. Remove 10gm of standard Art Clay Silver from the package and roll into a ball.

3. Roll the clay over the texture plate to a thickness of 1.5mm. Cut an approximately. 1" square from the clay and remove excess. While still on the texture plate, take the edge of one of the plastic slats and press into each side of the square, making an indented frame around the outside edge.

4. Place a small amount of olive oil on the end of the carved heart stamp and carefully impress a heart deeply into each of the square's four corners.

5. Grip the fired gold heart with a tweezers and drop into the middle of the silver clay square, centering it. Press very slightly into the damp clay. Remove the silver and gold clay square from the texture plate by bending the plate and lifting the silver clay gently. Place on a flat nonstick surface.

6. Using the Syringe Type and a green tip, draw a fine bead of silver clay around the edge of the gold heart, capturing it and filling in the gaps with Paste Type. Smooth with a damp paint-

Gold Foil Embossing

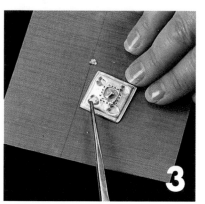

Gold Foil Embossing

Gold Foil Embossing

brush.

7. With the tip of a file or similar tool, create a dotted design outside the gold heart edge. Dry thoroughly.

8. Use files and 600 and 1200 grit sandpapers to smooth and even all edges and top of pendant.

9. Gently place fiber blanket over top of piece and invert. Place on flat surface.

10. Using a small amount of syringe and/or Paste Type, attach the bailback to the top of the pendant, covering the tabs well. Allow to dry completely.

11. Place right side up on fiber blanket and fire at 1600°F for 10 minutes. Cool.

12. Brush well with stainless steel brush.

IV. Gold Foil Embossing

1. Using a paper punch, make four small hearts out of the gold foil. Make sure each fits into one of the impressed hearts on the face of the silver pendant. Trim the foil if necessary.

2. Heat kiln to 1472°F and program to hold there.

3. Dilute the white craft glue with a couple drops of water and place a dot of glue in each of the recessed heart wells. Drop a foil heart into each well, pressing lightly to adhere.

4. Set the pendant on a piece of fiberboard and load into the kiln.

5. When the kiln returns to 1472°F, time for 2 minutes.

6. At the end of the 2 minutes, remove the fiberboard with tongs and a protective glove. Immediately, position the pendant on the edge of the board with tweezers and burnish each heart firmly with the tip of the agate burnisher, including the edges. If the piece cools and the edges are still not adhered, you may repeat the heating up process, allowing the kiln to return to 1472°F before again timing for 2 minutes.

7. Once the gold foil hearts are firmly attached, and the piece has cooled, complete the polishing process using burnisher or sandpapers to a mirror finish. Polish with Wenol and soft cloth.

GLOSSARY

Annealing (glass)

The process of gradual cooling of the outside and the inside of the hot glass to assure that the glass won't cool too fast causing cracks or breaks. The temperature range starting at the softening point and ending at the strain point is generally located between 1100°F and 600°F (593°C and 316°C), depending on the chemical makeup of the particular glass.

Bail

A finding that attaches a pendant to a necklace.

Bezel setting

A way of setting a stone in which the stone is held by a band of metal around the outside of the stone.

Binder

A cementing medium; either a material added to the powder to increase the green strength of the compact, and which is expelled during sintering; or a material (usually of relatively lower melting point) added to a powder mixture for the specific purpose of cementing together powder particles which alone would not sinter into a strong body.

Bisque

Unglazed porcelain or ceramics that have been fired, probably only once. They may be fragile. The term is also used to describe the body underneath a glaze.

Brass

Copper-based alloys in which zinc is the principal added element. Brass is harder and stronger than either of its alloying elements copper or zinc; it is malleable and ductile; develops high tensile with cold-working and not heat treatable for purposes of hardness development.

Brushed finish

Brushed finishes are made by rubbing a stiff metal brush across the metal surface of jewelry, slightly reducing the metal's reflectivity.

Cabochon, en

A stone that has a rounded, domed surface with no facets.

Ceramics

Defined as products made from inorganic materials having non-metallic properties, usually processed at a high temperature at some time during their manufacture. The word "ceramics" comes from the Greek word "Keramos" meaning "Pottery," "Potter's Clay," or "a Potter."

Coefficient of Expansion (COE)

The COE is a number determined by a scientific formula measuring the expansion and contraction of the glass during heating and cooling. The measured expansion of heated glass based on the percentage of change of a glass rod heated one degree centigrade.

Corundum

A very hard mineral (hardness 9); only diamond is harder. Corundum is called ruby or sapphire, depending on the color (which depends on which metallic oxides are present). In its rare pure form, corundum is colorless and called white sapphire. Rubies contain chromic oxide, blue sapphires contain titanium, yellow sapphires contain ferric oxide. Other impure forms are opaque.

Cubic Zirconium (also known as CZ)

CZ is an inexpensive, lab-produced gemstone that resembles a diamond. Cubic zirconia was developed in 1977.

Culet
> The bottom point of a gemstone or a small facet that is ground at the base of a brilliant-cut gemstone. The culet prevents splintering of the stone. Modern stones rarely have a faceted culet.

Devitrification
> (1) The process whereby glass becomes partly crystallized as it cools (usually too slowly) from the molten state; (2) the crystals formed by this process. Devitrification may also occur on the surface as a result of the unstable composition of the glass, unsuccessful annealing or accidental firing.

Dichroic glass
> Glass that has been coated with a thin layer of metallic oxide. Dichroic coatings transmit certain wavelengths of light while reflecting others, creating an interference effect similar to iridescence.

Eyepin (screw-eye)
> An eyepin is a thin wire with a loop at one end; it is used for linking beads together.

Facet
> One of the flat surfaces of a cut stone or glass.

Finding
> The parts that jewelers use in making jewelry. For example, clasps, hooks, pin backs, jump rings, and earring backs are findings.

Fire scale
> Caused by oxygen combining with copper present in the silver-copper alloy. A sterling silver alloy contains 925 parts out of a thousand parts silver, and 75 parts out of a thousand parts copper. When the alloy is exposed to oxygen in the air at higher temperatures during annealing or soldering procedures, the copper at the surface is converted to Cu_2O (cuprous oxide), which has a reddish color, then to cupric oxide, CuO, which is black. It is, however, not just the metal at the very surface that is affected but deep inside the metal as well. Silver has the ability to absorb oxygen at high temperatures and conduct the oxygen to the interior of the metal itself where it can bond with copper atoms present thus causing deep firescale to occur.

Firing ceramics
> Baked in a hot oven or kiln. High firing (1200°C to 1400°C) is used for porcelain, moderate firing (1200°C to 1280°C) is used for stoneware, low firing (800°C to 1100°C) for earthenware.

Florentine finish
> A Florentine finish on a metal's surface reduces the metal's reflectivity. It is accomplished by engraving parallel lines into the surface using a sharp tool, and then making more lines or curves at right angles (cross-hatching).

Girdle
> The girdle is the widest perimeter of a gemstone.

Greenware
> Unfired, bone-dry clay objects.

Inclusions
> An inclusion is a particle of foreign matter contained within a mineral.

Karat (abbreviated Kt)
> A karat is a measure of the fineness of gold. 24 karat gold is pure gold. 18 karat gold is 18/24 gold (about 75 percent gold).

Liver of Sulfur

Potassa sulphurata (a mixture of various compounds of potassium and sulfur made by fusing potassium carbonate and sulfur).

Mohs Scale

The Mohs Scale of Hardness measures a substance's hardness, that is, how resistant it is to being scratched. In the Mohs scale, which ranges from 1 to 10, one substance is harder than another if it can scratch it. For example, a diamond (hardness = 10) will scratch garnet (hardness = 6.5-7.5), but not the other way around, so a diamond is harder than garnet. This scale was invented by Austrian mineralogist Friedrich Mohs (1773-1839).

Porcelain

Especially fine kind of pottery, fired at very high temperature. Usually high quality, hard, dense, white, non-porous, and if thin, translucent. Good porcelain rings when struck, a bad piece or cracked piece will not ring.

Sgraffito

A decoration that is achieved by scratching through a surface of slip or glaze to the body underneath.

Sintering

The metallurgical bonding of particles in a powder mass or compact resulting from a thermal treatment at a temperature below the melting point of the main constituent.

Spinel

A very hard semi-precious stone composed of octahedral crystals. Spinel ranges in color from red to black to yellow, frequently resembling rubies. Iron and chrome are components of spinel, giving it its color. Spinel belongs to the feldspar species and is found in Burma, Sri Lanka, and Thailand. Some varieties include: Balas ruby (red spinel), Almandine spinel (purple-red), Rubicelle (orange), Sapphire spinel (blue), Ghanospinel (blue), Chlorspinel (green). Spinel is also laboratory synthesized. Spinel has a hardness of 8.

Sterling Silver

A silver alloy that contains 92.5 percent silver and 7.5 percent copper. It can be worn by most. Sterling silver does tarnish with time.

Stress

A force creating tension and compression within glass that could cause unwanted breakage. Internal stress can be caused by poor annealing or fusing of incompatible glass.

Table

The table is the large, flat area at the top of a cut gemstone.

Thermal shock

Is caused by a sudden shift of temperature (hot or cold), causing the glass to break, crack or shatter.

Thermocouple

The temperature sensing probe of a pyrometer. It's inserted into the kiln chamber to measure temperature.

Vermeil

Gold-plated silver. Less occasionally, gold-plated bronze is referred to as vermeil.

About the Author

Jackie Truty, Art Clay World, USA

Jackie readily admits that her past experiences have had a great deal of influence on her current life's path. Once an operating room nurse and nurse manager, Jackie began working in flat, copper foiled glass as a hobby. Soon she moved to warm glass, fusing and slumping a variety of shapes and showing her work in art shows and galleries in Michigan, Illinois, New York, and Georgia. When she finally settled on fusing glass for jewelry full time, she began studying the mechanics of dichroic glass, researching its beginnings and ultimately writing a book, published in 2002. Wire wrapping seemed to be the next, natural step to accompany the dichroic glass, and she began to sell her wire-sculpted glass in jewelry shows and teach wire sculpting and fused dichroic glass in her home studio. In 2000, she added lapidary arts to her repertoire after attending William Holland School for Lapidary Arts, and spent three weeks the following year digging and mining opal in Lightning Ridge and Yowah, Australia.

It was also in 2000 when Jackie saw a demonstration on metal clay that she knew she'd finally found her niche. Taking introductory and then back-to-back certification classes in the Autumn of 2000, she soon became a Senior Instructor in Art Clay. Then in March of 2001, she accepted a position as one of two Directors of Education, flying to Japan for her Masters training. In December 2002, she and the past President of Art Clay USA, Inc., Seigo Mukoyama, joined forces to form a partnership and moved their newly-acquired business, Art Clay World, USA, from Torrance, California, to Oak Lawn, Illinois, where she runs the day-to-day operations as President.

These days, even with her 23 year-old daughter out on her own, and her husband of 25 years busy with the O'Hare Airport Expansion controversy, Art Clay World, USA, leaves Jackie little time for personal creativity. She continues to teach glass fusing annually at Glass Craft Expo in Las Vegas, and tours the United States teaching, demonstrating, and representing Art Clay. Jackie is committed to increasing awareness and acceptance of metal clay generally, and Art Clay specifically, as a valid artistic medium.

Index

Appendix

Art Clay World, USA
SELECTED GEMSTONE CHARACTERISTICS

SPECIES	HARDNESS (MOHS)	SPECIFIC GRAVITY	REFRACTIVE INDEX	DISPERSION	DURABILITY
Alabaster	1-1.5	2.2-2.4	1.52	med-high	low
Alexandrite*	8	3.68-3.78	1.75	low	high
Amber	2.5	1.03-1.1	1.54	none	low
Apatite	5	3.16-3.22	1.64-1.65	low	medium
Aquamarine	7.75	2.68-2.7	1.57-1.575	low	high
Azurite	3.5	3.8	1.48-1.65	none	low
Beryl	7.75	2.70	1.58	low	high
Cat's Eye*	8	3.68-3.79	1.54-1.75	low	high
Chalcedony	7	2.65	1.55	low	high
Chrysoberyl*	8.5	3.71	1.75	low	high
Corundum*	9			low	high
Diamond	10	3.52	2.42	high	high
Emerald*	7.75	2.66-2.78	1.56	low	high
Epidote	6	3.25-3.49	1.73-1.76	med-high	high
Feldspar	6-6.5			low	medium
Garnet*	7.5	3.7-4.16	1.74-1.89	med-high	high
Gypsum	1-1.5	2.3	1.53	med-high	low
Hematite**	5.5-6.5	4.95-5.3	2.94-3.22	none	high
Jade	6.5-7	3.30-3.38	1.68	none	high
Jadite	7	3.33	1.66	none	high
Jet	3.5	1.1-1.4	1.64-1.68	none	low
Kunzite	7	3.13-3.31	1.66-1.68	medium	low
Labradorite**	6	2.7-2.72	1.52	medium	medium
Lapis Lazuli	5	2.76-2.94	1.5	none	medium
Malachite	3-4	3.7-4	1.87-1.98	none	low
Marble	3	2.71	1.48-1.65	none	low
Moonstone**	6	2.5-2.55	1.52-1.54	low	high
Nephrite	6.5	2.96	1.62	none	high
Obsidian**	6	2.33-2.6	1.48-1.51	high	medium
Olivine	6	3.3-3.5	1.65	medium	high
Opal	6	1.97-2.2	1.45	none	low
Peridot**	6.5	3.34	1.68	low	medium
Quartz	7	2.65	1.55	low	high
Rodonite	5	3.53	1.73-1.74	none	medium
Ruby*	9	4.00	1.77	low	high
Sapphire*	9	4.00	1.77	low	high
Serpentine	3.5	2.5-2.7	1.57	low	low
Sodalite	5	2.13-2.29	1.483	low	medium
Spectrolite**	6	2.7-2.72	1.52	low	medium
Sphene	5	3.45-3.56	1.95-2.05	high	medium
Spinel*	8	3.60	1.72	low	high
Spodumene	7	3.18	1.66	low	low
Steatite	1-1.5	2.7-2.8		none	low
Topaz	8	3.54	1.63	low	medium
Tourmaline	7	3.06	1.63	low	high
Turquoise	5	2.6-2.8	1.61-1.65	none	medium
Zircon	7	4.02	1.81	high	high

* can be safely fired in place with Regular or Slow Dry Art Clay silver if not containing flaws
** can be fred with Art Clay Silver 650 Low Fire